Traction on The Grand

The Story of Electric Railways along Ontario's Grand River Valley

by John Mills

A **Railfare**  Book

ISBN 0-919130-27-5

Contents

Acknowledgements

BMcC: W. Bruce McCarvell, Guelph.
CPEL: Canadian Pacific Electric Lines, Preston.
CPR: Canadian Pacific Railway, Montreal.
HEPC: Ontario Hydro, Toronto.
JDK: J.D. Knowles, Toronto.
JMM: Author collection.
JRM: J.R. McFarlane, Portland, Maine.
KWR: Kitchener-Waterloo "Record" or
     Kitchener-Waterloo Railways.
LGB: L.G. Baxter, Toronto.
NB: N. Bradshaw (from E.J. Freyseng, Toronto)
NM: Neil McCarten, Toronto.
OPM: O.P. Maus, Brantford.
RJS: R.J. Sandusky, Mississauga.
RRB: Robert R. Brown, Montreal.
RTS: Regina Transit System.
WCJ: W.C. Janssen, Chicago.
WE: W. Ernst, Preston.
WEM: W.E. Miller, Galt.
WM: W. Malcolm, Hamilton.
WH: Wm. Houston, Kitchener.

Preface

This book, the third in a series, concentrates on the electric lines of the part of Southern Ontario adjacent to the Grand River (plus a corporate outpost at Woodstock). Naturally fertile and prosperous, this area attracted early settlement which coalesced around two points: the head of river navigation at Brantford, and the water-power sites at and north of Galt. The latter gave rise to a densely-settled triangle bounded by Galt, Waterloo and Guelph, with outliers to the north at the Elmira and Fergus areas. Such conditions were ideal for the development of local railway transportation which appeared as expected: horse-car lines were built at an early date in Brantford and Berlin/Waterloo, and the Galt Preston & Hespeler was one of the first interurban lines in Canada. The vitality of the lines, particularly those in the northerly triangle, was thus established, and it continued for many years: the transformation of the G.P.&H. into the Grand River Railway in the early twenties was the most complete reconstruction in Canadian traction history.

As with the author's other books, the basic research for this one was done in the University of Toronto Library's comprehensive collections. Essential flesh was added to the bones by such knowledgeable friends as Mr. Orin Maus of Brantford (who placed a lifetime of research at the author's disposal), Mr. William Houston of Kitchener, Mr. W.E. Miller of Galt and Mr. B. McCarvell of Guelph. A fascinating day was spent delving into the remote recesses of the old Preston office building which produced a great deal of useful information, but unfortunately revealed that most rolling-stock and shop records had been destroyed some years before. Many fine photos (far more indeed than could be used) were supplied as noted in the captions of each photo. Information and encouragement was also given by many other individuals; no author could function without this support. My personal gratitude is also extended to Railfare Enterprises Limited for having rescued this book from the doldrums into which it threatened to decline, and for giving reason to hope that further volumes of this series will appear in due course.

Toronto, March 1977   J.M. Mills

1

Galt, Preston & Hespeler Street Railway, Grand River Railway

Car 23, the first double-truck car of the Galt Preston & Hespeler. (RJS from WE)

This was one of the earliest interurban electric lines in Canada, and was for many years one of the most energetic and progressive. The Galt & Preston Street Railway Co. was organized in 1890 for the purpose of hauling freight as well as passengers, a most unusual intention for the time. The Galt newspaper predicted, correctly, in October 1890,

"As the promoters of the line intend that it shall carry freight as well as passengers, its construction will give Preston splendid connection with the C.P.R."

Activities began early in 1894 when the line was built from the Grand Trunk station, Galt, north to Hunter's Corner, where it turned north-west along King and Main streets in Preston, a distance of 4-3/4 miles. 56 lb. relay rails on cedar ties were used. All trackage was on the street except on Concession St. and between Hunter's Corner and Cedar St., Preston, where it was beside the road. There was a 5% grade northbound on Water St. in Galt, and a short branch to the C.P.R. left the main line on this hill, having a curve of 100-foot radius on a 6.6% grade. Needless to say, alternative connections were soon provided.

Car 22, the other
original car. (WEM)

On King St.,
Preston, at the end of the line.
Little is known of these
open single-truck motor cars. (WEM)

23 hauling 25, one of the ex-Brooklyn trailers, in Galt. (WEM)

4

Electrification was supervised by Ahern and Soper, Ottawa, who installed Westinghouse equipment. The power house was a converted building at Lowther St. in Preston, the boilers and reciprocating engines being by the local Goldie & McCulloch firm.

NEW CARS

Two cars were built by the Ottawa Car Co., and were numbered 22 and 23 for reasons unexplained. No. 22 was a small single-truck street car and 23 was a double-truck combine with space for "small freight". Three open cars came second-hand from Brooklyn, N.Y. and were rebuilt as trailers by Patterson & Corbin, St. Catharines, before reaching Galt. The following is from a contemporary newspaper account:

"For several days past President Todd and Secretary Lutz, of the Galt & Preston Street Railway Co., have been anxiously a-waiting the arrival of the electric motor cars from Ottawa, and when it was learned yesterday afternoon that they were between Toronto and Galt, quite a crowd repaired to the C.P.R. station in the evening to await the arrival of the train with the cars. It came in about 9 o'clock. The cars are well equipped and made after the most modern style. No. 23 is a 40 ft. car, containing a baggage compartment, which takes up 10 feet of the space. The seats are finely upholstered; bevelled glass windows decorate the ends and the car contains four electric heaters. Fourteen incandescent electric lights,

with very pretty globes, hang from the ceiling, and the car has a seating capacity for about 30 passengers. Car No. 22 is about 18 feet long, has also four heaters, and seats run lengthwise. The cars are attracting a great deal of admiration by all who have seen them, and are really a credit to the Company. The trailers are expected from St. Catharines any day now. The motors are being unloaded and placed on the track today and will likely be run to Preston tonight."

LINE OPENS

Trial trips began on July 21, 1894, and the line was officially opened five days later. The opening had been delayed for a time because the C.P.R. overpass in Galt had to be rebuilt to permit the electric cars to pass under. The ceremonial decorated car on July 26 started from the G.T.R. station in Galt and ran to the temporary end of track at the Speed River in Preston. Tracks had been laid beyond the river to the hotels but the bridge was not ready for another six weeks. (Preston Springs had a reputation for the curative properties of its spring waters, and several large resort hotels were established as a result.)

To handle the freight business, the Company used a Baldwin "steam dummy" obtained from an unknown source. Apparently this 0-4-0 engine was not powerful enough, for in 1897 the company purchased a larger "dummy", No. 4 of the Hamilton & Dundas St. Ry. Used only a few months before the H.&D. was electrified, it remained in Hamilton inactive from 1897 until 1902 when, owing to the Hamilton influence in Preston & Berlin affairs at that time, it went into service at Preston, perhaps on construction but certainly as motive power for the temporary passenger trains. It did not run on the G.P.&H. until all P.&B. assets were turned over in 1903. No trace of the 1894 G.P.&H. steam dummy has been found and its origin, life and disposal remain obscure.

The company was required by its franchise to locate its carhouse and shops in Preston, and to meet all C.P.R. trains in Galt for Preston passengers.

Prosperity encouraged the company to further construction, and in 1895 it sold additional stock, bought two more cars, changed its name to Galt Preston & Hespeler St. Ry. and started building north-east along the Speed River. Rails reached Hespeler in January 1896, bringing route mileage to nine. A popular a-musement park, closed during World War I, was located at Idylwild, the mid-point of the Hespeler line, and another park was maintained briefly south of Preston.

By the end of 1896 the company was car-rying 35,000 passengers and 1,000 tons of freight a month, and it was stated that the freight business alone was paying the operating costs and interest. (Carload freight was handled by the "steam motor" at night, permitting the power plant to be shut down.) Much of the freight business was coal captured from the Grand Trunk by undercutting rates; the G.P. & H. at that time came under Provincial regu-lations as a street railway rather than, as was later the case, under Federal control. The G.T.R., restrained by regulations from reducing its rates beyond a certain figure, retaliated by providing free cartage to premises.

FREIGHT TRAFFIC

Two more cars were ordered from Ottawa in 1896. It seems likely that additional cars were acquired around the turn of the century, as there were 12 passenger motor cars on the roster in June 1904 whereas known orders account for only seven.

In 1898 improved interchange facilities were installed with the C.P.R. at Samuelson Street in Galt, which was on the opposite side of the C.P. line from the older Front St. spur, but had easier grades.

The first electric locomotive was built in 1903; this was equipped with standard air brakes and could safely handle longer trains than could the "steam motor". In April 1903 this engine when in use on construction work ran away on Preston hill and overturned on the Speed River bridge; fortunately there were no fatalities but one of those injured was M. W. Kirkwood, later General Manager.

1903 was a very important year in the history of the line. A long process of reor-ganization and integration with the Canadian Pacific system was begun; the Preston & Berlin line was opened (see below); freight facilities were improved and the first double-tracking was undertaken. The reorganization started as a complicated schedule of corporate moves, partly to consolidate C.P. control over the line and partly to further C.P. expansion in Western Ontario. Briefly, the C.P.R. incorporated the Berlin Waterloo Wellesley & Lake Huron Ry. with power to build a line through Berlin and Mount Forest to Goderich and Wiarton. Certain internal agreements in effect unified the G.P. & H. and P. & B. under the name of the former and both companies were leased to the C.P.R. effective January 1, 1908.

The Canadian Pacific's ambitions in the direction of Lake Huron were, as it happened, carried out by other means, so that the ex-tension provisions of the new charter were not used. The Grand River Railway name was substituted for the older name in 1918 when in a final reorganization, a C.P. Vice-President became G.R.R. President, the G.P. & H. Pres-ident becoming G.R.R. Vice-President. The B.W.W.& L.H. had been legally renamed Grand River Railway several years before but the new name was not generally used at first.

Locomotive 10 was the ancestor, through two drastic rebuildings, of G.R.R. motor 222 (WEM).

PRESTON & BERLIN

The impetus for the formation of this railway came from the irrepressible John Patterson of Hamilton Cataract fame. The company had been organized in 1894 but was dormant until 1900 when it was reorganized with Patterson as President, and T.M. Todd of the G.P.&H. as Vice-President. The route as eventually built started at a G.P.&H. connection at East Preston, and went around the back of the town to Joseph St. where it connected with the Hespeler line. This new line paralleled the G.P.&H. King St. trackage and was obviously intended for freight service as it lacked the heavy grades and street running of the older line; it was apparently only for convenience that it was built under the P.&B. rather than the G.P.&H. name.

From Preston Jct. the P.&B. line climbed a long curving 2% grade to the higher land at Hagey's Siding, and thence through Freeport and Centreville and along King St., Berlin, to a connection with the Berlin & Waterloo St. Ry. at Albert St. (now Madison Ave.) From this point P.&B. cars used B.&W. rails to reach Water St. downtown. There was a small amount of street running on Railway St. in Preston, but this was converted to private right-of-way in 1920 by the simple expedient of moving the street, not the track. A long bridge over the Grand River at Freeport had four 140-foot spans, and was the most scenic spot on the line.

The Hamilton Radial Electric Railway was instrumental in the early days of the line, but its influence ended early in 1903 probably because attempts by "The Cataract" to buy control of the G.P.&H. had failed. (In July 1900 the P.&B. Co. transferred all its assets to the H.R.E.R. which transferred them back again in April 1903, at which time the G.P.& H. leased the P.&B.) The G.P.&H. was closely involved in the P.&B. project, as the C.P.R. intended to use it as a freight feeder, but early construction drawings (in the O.E.R. H.A. Archives) bear the Hamilton Radial name. To further confuse the situation, the C.P.R. was understood to be interested in purchasing "The Cataract" so it is probably now impossible to determine the extent of any one company's influence over any of the others.

Tracklaying on the P.&B. was virtually complete in 1902, using 71-lb. rail imported from Belgium. However, there was a delay in fitting out the new Preston power house and a substation in Berlin. Accordingly, a passenger service was begun on February 5, 1903 using the G.P.&H. "steam motor" and second-hand trailers whose nature is unknown. The official inauguration of electric traction as far as Berlin was on August 21, 1903 but normal service did not begin for another five days.

The Waterloo extension began not from the end of the line at Albert St., but rather from Cedar Grove at the point where the rails entered onto King St. This line ran around Berlin and split near Queen St. One branch veered sharply into the centre of Berlin to a freight yard at Joseph St., while the other ended at another yard at Erb St. in Waterloo. There was some street running on both these branches. Service through to Waterloo began on October 6, 1904. In 1908 the Preston & Berlin was formally amalgamated with the G.P.&H. and the rest of this account concerns the united company.

FURTHER DEVELOPMENT

Returning to 1903, another car was ordered, and the G.P.&H. undertook to provide cars and operate the P.&B. as an integral part of the system on completion. All cars apparently belonged legally to the G.P.&H. but a proportion were lettered for the P.&B. A station was built at Preston Jct. and in 1904 G.P.&H. freight trains began using the P.&B. line via Joseph St. in Preston. To make this possible, the junction between the Hespeler branch and the main line, formerly a sharp curve east of the Speed River, was relocated on a curved trestle over the river. The old connection, was, however, also retained until a building was erected across the King St. frontage about 1919.

The roadside tracks between Hunter's Corner and East Preston, which were now carrying bith P.&B. and G.P.&H. freight traffic as well as frequent passenger cars, were doubled in 1903 and a new freight interchange, the third in ten years, was built parallel to the G.T.R. leaving the main line at Hunter's Corner and terminating in a 3-track yard perpendicular to the C.P.R. Access to the steam line was via the yard wye. This new yard was expanded steadily over the years until at the end of the electric era it included 7 interchange tracks and four G.R.R. classification tracks. In addition, much of the C.P.R. yard was electrified.

With the building of the Berlin line, a new power house was opened near the Speed River and the machinery moved there from the Lowther St. building. Four years later the generating capacity was increased by the addition of a more powerful Corliss-type engine directly connected to a larger generator. The new power house was much the oldest structure on the line as it was one of the earliest large homes in the area, dating from about 1845. The railway gutted the interior and rebuilt it (with a new roof) to accommodate the engines and generators, adding a structure on the rear to hold the furnaces and boilers.

In 1905 a second barn was built at Preston and two new cars ordered, but at 3:00 A.M. on December 4, 1906 the barn was destroyed by fire.

PRESTON BARN BURNS

"Preston was visited by one of the most disastrous fires in its history at an early hour this morning, when the large main car barn and the rolling stock of the G.P.&H. and the P.&B. St. Ry. Companies were completely gutted by the flames.

The fire was first noticed by Preston's night watchman about 2 o'clock who at first thought that the workmen were engaged in repairing cars, but on a second look saw that flames were coming out of the upper windows.

While the watchman was sending in the alarm other citizens were attracted by the bright reflection in the skies, and in a few minutes nearly the entire population of Preston was on the scene and witnessed the flames devouring the valuable rolling stock of this company, which has become the pride of Preston, Galt, Hespeler, Berlin and Waterloo.

When the firemen arrived the flames had secured such headway and the material in the interior of the barns was such easy prey for the burning element that their work was next to hopeless.

The barns were situated adjacent to the powerhouse and junction station, and the firemen confined their attention to saving these buildings as well as the skating rink on the opposite side.

The two large and valuable coaches Nos. 20 and 30, the two summer open cars, the Dominion Express Co.'s car, two G.P.&H. cars and the new $12,000 freight motor were in the building when the doors were closed shortly after midnight, and this morning all that remained were the trucks and rails on which the cars had been standing, which had fallen through to the basement.

The smaller shed on the easterly side contained the trailers and this building was saved.

The Company had two small closed cars in the yards, the vestibule of one of which was scorched, and these are giving a two-hour service between Berlin, Hespeler and Galt.

President Todd, Secretary Lutz and Manager Clemens were busy this morning telegraphing for the loan of cars and were successful in securing one from the B.&W. Co., and will secure larger cars from the Toronto, Hamilton and Buffalo.

"The total loss is estimated at $60,000 and the insurance on the sheds and cars that were destroyed will amount to $41,000.

The Company confidently expects to re-

Car 20, burnt at Preston
when only a few months old. (RJS from WE)

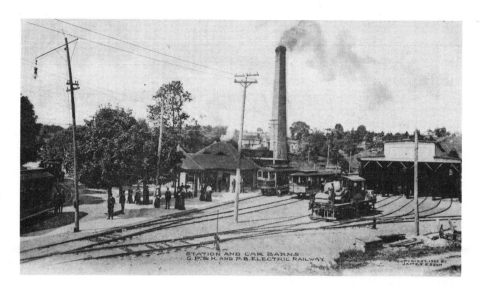

Preston Jct. in 1905 before the fire. Note motor 10 piled high with what looks like bags of feed; behind it seems to be one or more of the open trailers. The heavy open car next to the station is unknown; perhaps one of "the two summer open cars" burnt. (BMcC)

store the regular service in a few days, and will place orders immediately for new cars similar to those that were destroyed.

The re-erection of the barns will commence at once.

The cause of the fire is unknown, but it is thought that it might have started from a stove in one of the cars." (contemporary newspaper account)

Destroyed in the fire were six passenger cars, including the two newest ones, two freight cars and a sweeper. Only two passenger cars and a freight car escaped the flames, but one of the freight cars was returned to service (being confusingly given the number of one of the burned passenger cars) as was the sweeper. The identity of the passenger cars that survived is unfortunately not certain. Four new cars were ordered from Ottawa and these are the first passenger cars whose history can be traced with certainty. A large freight motor was also built at this time. In 1910 two more cars came from the Ottawa Car Co. and a second slightly smaller freight motor was ordered. The arrival of this engine permitted the ex-Dundas "steam motor" to be disposed of. (The number of cars owned, as deduced

Car 21 in 1910. One of the four cars built immediately after the Preston fire. (WEM)

Car 51 on the Hespeler branch trestle at Preston Jct. Note mainline trestle on left, replaced in 1924 (WCJ).

from the newspaper clipping, cannot be reconciled with the number of cars as noted in Government statistical reports.)

FREIGHT CONNECTIONS

Local merchants were pressing for connection to the Grand Trunk as well as with the C.P.R., but in 1908 the Board of Railway Commissioners refused to make such an order. The picture changed, however, and in 1914 connection with the G.T.R. was established at three points: Hunter's Corner, East Preston and Erb St., Waterloo. The Galt "West Side Freight Spur" was built in 1910, crossing the Grand River on a private bridge and turning south along side streets to serve a number of small industries. Grades and curvature were very severe on this branch.

Starting in April 1911, Niagara power was supplied by Ontario Hydro, and the Preston steam plant, expanded only four years before, was placed in reserve. (It was reopened at least once, during a severe power shortage in 1918). In the following year the franchises covering street operation in both Galt and Preston expired. Both were renewed, in Galt for 10 years and in Preston for 25. New freight stations were built at Erb St. and at Guelph St. in Preston, and two more cars came from the Preston Car & Coach Co. About this time 65-lb. rail replaced the early 56-lb. material on much of the Hespeler branch.

In 1914 the street trackage on King St. in Preston was converted to double track and was centred on the street between East Preston and Cedar St. where it had previously been laid beside the road.

NUMBERING OF CARS

Here we must digress to comment on the peculiar numbering systems used by the Canadian Pacific electric lines. After the 1906 fire, the new cars obtained were numbered 21, 31, 41 and 51; however the two 1910 cars were 61 and 81 (why no 71?) while to further confuse matters, the 1912 cars were 205 and 215. In 1915 the L.E.& N. cars continued the 200-series in steps of 10, but in 1921 everything was changed again. In this new scheme, all digits of L.E.& N. vehicle numbers were odd, while all G.R.R. digits were even; "0" and "1" were not ordinarily used by either railway. The result was that when the 1915 cars were renumbered in 1921 they became 933, 935, 937, 939, 953 and 955. It will be seen that, following the above rules, 933 was the first number in the 900-series that could be used. The observant number-collector will have remembered later G.R.R. locomotives 230, 232 and 234. However, these were acquired in 1946, by which time, presumably, the creators of this remarkable scheme had passed from the scene and nobody noticed that they should have been 242, 244 and 246.

In September 1917, M.N. Todd, President of the G.P.& H. and Vice-President of the L.E.& N., died at Galt. His father, T.M. Todd, had been promoter and first President

Right: Motor 20 as built.
1908 (RJS from WE)

Below: Freeport bridge over
the Grand River, about
1910. (WEM)

Right: Preston Junction,
from a post card mailed
in 1915 (BMcC)

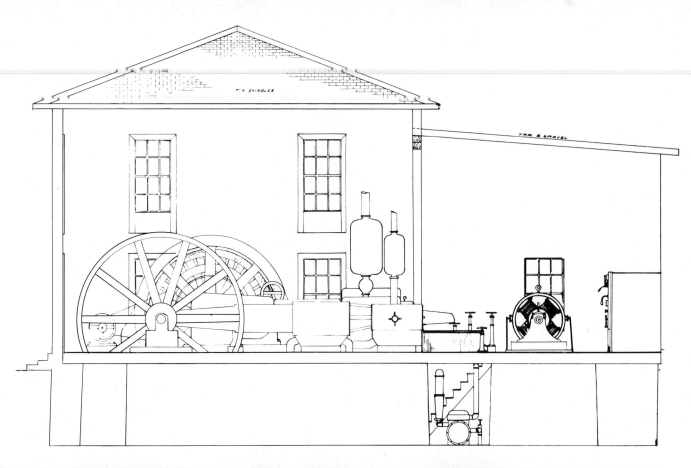

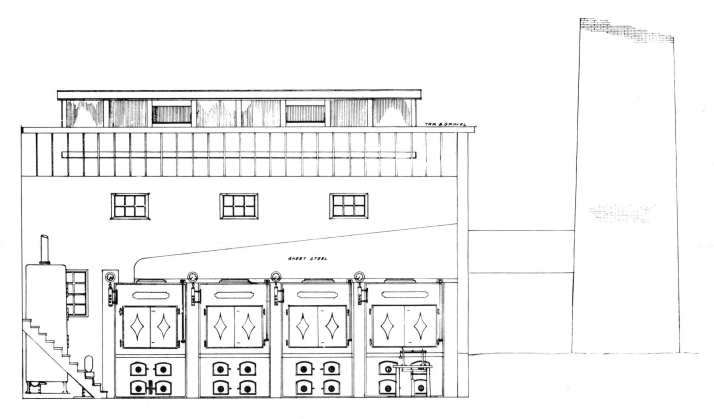

Above: A cross-section (taken from a contemporary print) of the second Galt power house showing the engines in the former manor house and the furnaces in a separate structure joined to it. In the illustration, the huge flywheel should be noted. This was needed to smooth out the power of the reciprocating engines. (CPEL)

Below: A view of Car 23, possibly taken at the Ottawa Car Company plant. (JMM)

Left: Car 51 at the junction between main line (right) and Hespeler branch (straight ahead), Joseph St., Preston (NM). Below: 215 posed outside the Preston Car plant, 1912.(WH)

A famous shot of car 61 at the Preston plant. The problem is that the car so carefully posed by the postcard photographer was built not by Preston but by Ottawa. It has been suggested that the order was placed with Preston but sub-contracted to Ottawa, and this is plausible since 1910 was a very busy year for the new company. (JMM)

of the G.P. & H. and his son, M.N. Todd, succeeded to both his posts. The son was then 24 years old and was said to be the youngest railroad President in Canada. M.W. Kirkwood (who had been on staff since 1894 when he supervised the fitting-out of the first power house) was promoted from Superintendent to General Manager of both lines.

SHOPS EXPANDED

In 1918 most of the line between Preston and Kitchener was relaid with 85-lb. rail and the displaced stock was used in a two-mile diversion of the Hespeler line in which the track was moved back from the river and straightened. Previously it had often been closed down by spring floods. In the same year the Preston carhouse was remodelled and enlarged with additional maintenance and storage space, including an extremely complete outfit of machine tools. The Baldwin type trucks for all the 1921 steel cars were made here by railway forces, who also did much of the detail work on the bodies, even to the point of designing and casting the interior lighting fixtures. They also finished off the new locomotives from body shells by Preston, and manufactured most of the overhead line fittings required for the 1921 rebuilding.

On April 7, 1918 locomotive 10 was badly damaged by an oil-stove explosion at the C.P.R.

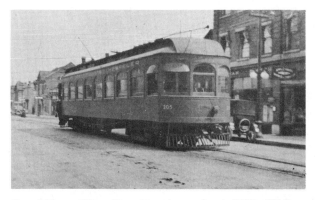

Car 205 on King St., Preston, about 1915 (WM)

Station, and was drastically rebuilt by Preston and transformed into G.R.R. motor 222.

The franchise for street operation on the outskirts of Kitchener expired in October 1919 and the Public Utilities Commission, owner of the Kitchener-Waterloo Railways, prepared to take over about 4700 feet of P. & B. track from Albert St. (Madison Ave.) to the City Limit. A new line was built by the G.R.R., starting at the city limit, by-passing the street section and rejoining the Waterloo line at Courtland St. A "temporary" wooden station (destined to last for twenty years) was built at Queen St. and opened on May 1, 1921 when regular G.R.R. service started running to this point instead of

Below: Five cars posed on Preston hill, just north of the carhouse, about 1912. (KWR)

Above: Car 844 southbound at Galt station about 1925 (CPEL)
Centre: 846 on the main line and 828 on the Hespeler branch at Preston, October 1942 (JDK)
Left: 844 ready to leave Galt about 1944 (JDK)

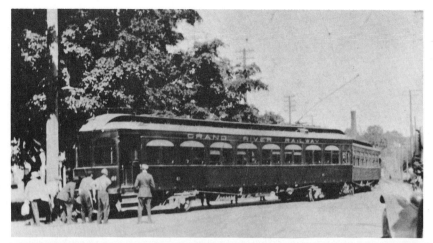

Car 61, bound for Galt, derailed just south of the Speed River bridge in Preston, 1918. (OPM)

to downtown Kitchener. A new station called Kitchener Junction was opened in October at the point where the new alignment left King St. A wye was installed (later made into a loop) for K.W. cars which now terminated here.

The Galt franchise also expired at this time, and here too a new line was built. This was a major piece of work, 1½ miles of double track. It crossed under the C.P.R. through the existing G.T.R. subway, and made an end-on connection with the L.E.&N. line.

The C.P.R. "Downtown Spur" and interchange had to be relocated and the C.P. freight shed, a large structure 200 x 40 feet, moved bodily sideways 40 feet in order to clear the new double track. A new connection to the C.P.R. station for passengers and express was also built, reaching the station from the east where the former Water St. connection (now abandoned) had approached from the west.

HIGH-VOLTAGE CONVERSION

This entire relocation was opened on February 1, 1921 and while constructed for 1500-volt operation, was operated at 600 volts until, on December 4 of the same year the entire Grand River Railway line was changed from 600-volt power. All the old cars were at once withdrawn and replaced by nine new steel cars and an express car, built by the Preston Car & Coach Co. They showed C.P. Railway influence strongly in their appearance, and could run in multiple with the 1915 L.E.&N. cars. Through trains were run both north and south of Galt, using a random mixture of G.R.R. and L.E.&N. cars which in actual fact formed a single pool of equipment.

As part of the same improvement programme, a new 1500-volt substation was built in Preston behind the former power house. Double track was constructed on the "freight line" from East Preston to the Guelph St. freight station, and from Preston Jct. 1¼ miles uphill to the site of Hagey's Siding. This helped eliminate delays caused by slow-moving freight trains on the long 2% grade. A new interurban station was opened in December 1923 at Main St. in Galt for use by both lines. This was built on the site of a former mill pond which was filled in.

In 1923 three of the newest G.P.&H. wooden cars were shopped at Preston and rebuilt to the new standards, emerging very different in appearance and converted for 1500 volts. It was intended that the fourth of the

Construction on the new double-track line in Galt, 1920 (CPEL)

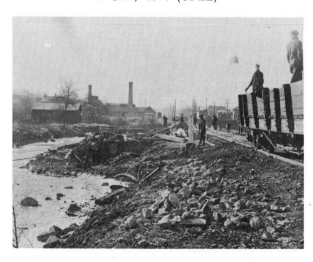

An official portrait of car 844 at Preston Junction about 1928. (CPEL)

1910-12 cars should also be rebuilt, but this was never done and the number which had been left for it (822) was not used. Possibly its mate, 824, was found unsatisfactory in its new guise as it was off the roster within ten years, but the two 1912 cars, as 826 and 828, survived until 1947. The four 1907 cars were to have become trailers but in fact were unused from 1921 until about 1935 when they were scrapped. 21 and 31 technically "belonged" to the G.R.R. and 41, 51 and 61 to the L.E.&N. They were to have been renumbered, respectively, 422, 424, 535, 537 and 533, but this was never done. (it will be noted that 61 had the distinction of having two numbers reserved for it, 822 and 533, neither of which it ever took.) A December 1921 inventory reveals that the lines together owned 3 cabooses, 3 boarding cars, 10 flat cars, 7 hopper ballast cars and a ballast spreader. Since they participated fully in interline freight arrangements, they did not require a separate group of revenue freight cars.

In 1924 the four spans of the Freeport bridge were replaced by heavier ones, and on November 10 of the same year a wider highway bridge was opened over the Speed River in Preston. Formerly, G.R.R. main line rails had crossed on a separate single-track wooden bridge, but double track was now carried across the road bridge. Freight and Hespeler branch trains continued to use their curving wooden trestle.

For historical reasons the Galt/Preston area was one of the few in Ontario where bus competition with electric cars was permitted. In order to protect its position, the G.R.R. began bus service between Galt and Preston on September 14, 1925. This replaced the former short Galt-Preston rail runs which had alternated with the hourly trains to Kitchener/Waterloo, giving half-hour service as far as Preston; the Waterloo runs were not affected by the bus service. In 1926 some bus runs were, however, extended to Kitchener where they ran via King and Queen streets to the G.R.R. station. Thus, by means of buses the railway re-introduced direct downtown service in Kitchener whcih had been given up on expiry of the rail franchise a few years before; the rail passenger service was thus placed at a

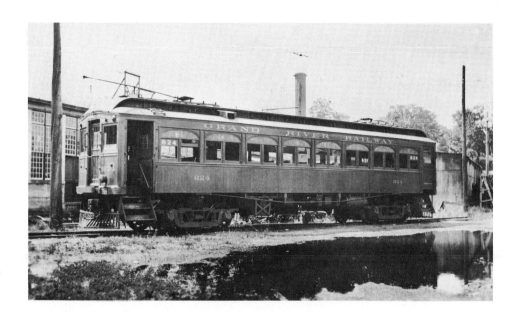

Right: Car 824
(formerly 81) as
rebuilt (OPM)

Below: 624
rebuilt from 866
after a fire (JMM)

Below: Interior of 842
(after post-war modernization)(RJS)
Lower right: Motor 228
near Hunter's Corner on the
1937-built double track
January 1960. (RJS)

Car 939 receives passengers for Kitchener
brought down from C.P.R. Sta. on 844, 1943 (JDK)

disadvantage.

In 1932 the company offices, formerly in rented quarters in Galt, were moved to the upper floor of the Preston shop, displacing the stores which moved elsewhere in the building. In the following year one of the 1921 steel cars (866) was gutted by fire, and when rebuilt was converted into a passenger-baggage combine and renumbered 624. This work was carried out at Preston shop and was so carefully done that no trace of its all-passenger origin could be seen.

During 1936 and 1937 the air whistles carried by the cars and engines were replaced by Westinghouse pneuphonic air horns whose melodious notes, tuned in a two-tone chime, will never be forgotten.

MORE RELOCATIONS

In 1937, after fifteen years of discussion, the last piece of roadside trackage, between Hunter's Corner and East Preston, was relocated along the Canadian National right-of-way as part of a highway-widening scheme. This project, unusually large for Depression years, was the result of a three-way agreement between the railway, the C.N.R., and the Ontario Department of Highways which bore the largest portion of the cost. The 1.8 miles of double track was opened on November 8, 1937.

On April 24, 1938 passenger service to Waterloo was discontinued and all trips terminated at Queen St. station in Kitchener, though for a time some commuter runs went as far as Glasgow St., Kitchener. Freight service to Waterloo was unaffected.

LAST STREET RUNNING

The franchise covering street running on King St. in Preston had now come to an end, and on August 27, 1939 operation on the streets of the town was discontinued. This was the last of the original route built in 1894, and had been used only by passenger cars since early in the century. The railway had now been entirely relocated from the highway to private right-of-way, a transformation often wished for, but rarely attained by interurban electric railways.

This also marked the end of the single snow sweeper. This ancient vehicle had not been converted for 1500 volts; it was required only on the paved trackage in Preston and could only be used at night after normal schedules had ended and the voltage in the wires of this section could be reduced to 600.

The passenger service was now diverted to the freight line, and congestion became acute on the 3/4 mile of single track remaining between Guelph St. and Joseph St. in Preston. Here, 52 passenger trains, 20 freight trains and ten switching moves were operated on a typical day. Therefore the track was doubled during the summer of 1940, as was the Hespeler branch between Preston station and Joseph St., completing a continuous double track for six miles from Main St., Galt, to Hagey's, with two minor breaks: the gauntlet track under the C.P.R. at Galt, and the single - track curved trestle at Preston Jct.; this station was now renamed simply Preston.

At this time the old Preston power plant was still just as it had been when closed down in 1920. The building now underwent a second transformation when the generating machinery was removed and the interior fitted up as office space for the Electric Lines. The staff moved here in May 1943 from its former quarters upstairs in the flat-roofed shop building, which had been exceedingly hot in summer and subject to roof leaks in all seasons. The inventory of generating machinery sold at this time is interesting: horizontal cross-compound Corliss-type engine rated at 750 H.P., 125 R.P.M., 120 lb. steam pressure built by Goldie & McCulloch in 1907. Directly connected to this was a 500-kw. 370-volt 3-phase 25-cycle Westinghouse generator dating from the same year. Also present was one tandem-compound Wheelock-type engine built by Goldie & McCulloch in 1904, rated at 350 H.P., 90 R.P.M.,

On the Hespeler branch at Joseph St., Preston. 826 (right) on July 4, 1946 and 937 (below) the following day (WCJ).

120-lb. pressure. "Generator formerly connected by belt to this unit was sold some years ago." The rear wing, added to the building in 1903 to house the furnaces and boilers, was demolished.

HEAVY FREIGHT TRAFFIC

Congestion at the C.P.R. interchange was becoming a serious problem. At first it was used only by cars bound for Grand River Railway points; cars for the L.E. & N. were delivered at Main St. over the "downtown spur" by a C.P.R. switcher. In February 1933, however, the C.P. eliminated its Galt switcher; freight for both railways began passing through the G.R.R. interchange, and the electric lines had to do the classification (sorting) of cars formerly done by the C.P.R.

By the beginning of 1940, the total freight business of the two electric lines was greater than at any time in their history, and by 1941 they were being called on to handle an average of 85 cars a day over interchange tracks having a maximum capacity of 42 cars. As a result, freight cars often had to be placed on the wye tracks, which were partially electrified, or left in the C.P. yard, which was not. The chaos

became so serious that the Kitchener freight train, due to leave Galt daily about 5:30 A.M., often did not get away before 10:00 A.M., by which time the full passenger schedule was in operation causing power troubles as well as delays and heavy expense in overtime wages.

Drastic changes were indicated, and in 1943 the entire interchange was rebuilt and two tracks of the C.P. yard electrified. In addition, the "Downtown Spur" and the C.P. freight station and yard tracks, located north of Main St. in Galt, were electrified and connected to the G.R.R. as well as the L.E. & N. line. The newly-electrified track totalled over two miles, but was still insufficient; over the next ten years five additional tracks were installed at the interchange, mostly for G.R.R. classification (i.e. sorting of cars by destination.)

In November 1943 a new and attractive brick station was opened at Queen St., Kitchener, replacing the ugly wooden building erected in 1921. Passenger business during the war was heavy, particularly with the cancellation of the auxiliary bus service. However the passenger cars were ample in number and well-maintained, so that conditions were not

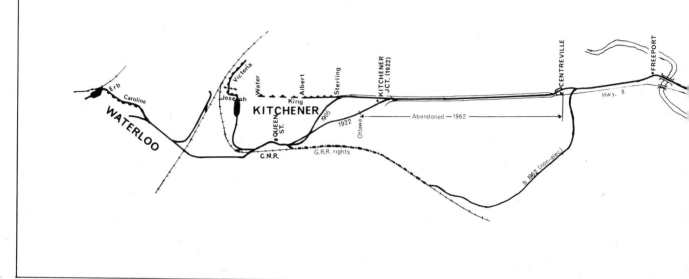

844 visits the two Kitchener stations. Right:
The old "temporary" station in 1940 (LGB)
Above: the new building in 1950 (JMM)

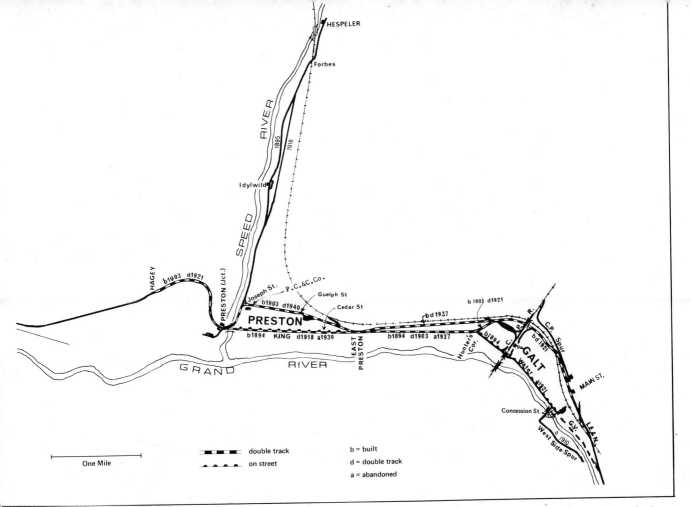

One Mile

double track
on street

b = built
d = double track
a = abandoned

as severe here as on some other lines. In June and again in August of 1943 the Electric Lines management requisitioned the C.P.R. for authority to purchase a new locomotive and two passenger cars. Authority was not received, but it is doubtful that new equipment could have been obtained at this time in any case. Nothing further was heard of the passenger cars, but plans for a new locomotive went ahead, and in July 1946 the steel frame for an engine, to be built at Preston, was delivered to the shops. It was not utilized, in view of the purchase of the Utah motors (see below) and was eventually taken to Montreal for disposition by the C.P.R.

POST-WAR YEARS

On December 30, 1946 the hourly Galt-Kitchener rail service was replaced by buses of Canadian Pacific Transport Ltd., (the special trips connecting with C.P.R. trains at Galt had been handled by road since the previous August). Passengers were directed to the C.P.T. bus parked just west of the station, but over on the other side a G.R.R. combine could be seen loading express and parcels, and

passengers could ride the electric car if they chose. A bus garage was built at Joseph St. as new equipment had crowded the space formerly used in the carhouse. In 1947 a town bus service was tried out in Preston but was discontinued as unprofitable.

Through tickets were sold from any point on the Electric Lines to and from any point on the Canadian Pacific system; railway enthusiasts visiting the lines found it helpful to purchase a reduced-rate C.P.R. "Weekend Return" ticket from Toronto to Port Dover via Galt, which was perfectly proper and cheaper than the ordinary return fare from Galt to Port Dover alone.

Despite the introduction of bus service, in 1946-47 all the steel cars were sent to the Angus Shops (Montreal) of the parent Canadian Pacific for reconditioning. New seat upholstery and a brighter interior paint scheme were applied, and the cars given more powerful motors and different gearing. This produced a decided improvement in speed which had been disappointingly low previously (maximum about

Canada's last interurban car, 626 southbound at Hagey, March 1955 (RJS)
Left below: Motors 232 and 333 on electrified C.P.R. track, Galt 1952
Right below: Motor 224 (formerly G.P.&H. 20) in 1928 (CPEL)

50 M.P.H.) A new automatic substation was installed at Simcoe on the L.E.&N. line, and three freight motors purchased from the abandoned Salt Lake and Utah line at Salt Lake City to cope with the increasing freight business, entering service as G.R.R. 230, 232 and 234. All the original freight motors were rebuilt in the postwar years; their tractive effort was increased, and most received more powerful motors.

In some ways the most surprising aspect of the postwar rehabilitation was the ordering, from National Steel Car Corp., Hamilton, of a new passenger-baggage combine body. This was the first new interurban car to be built in Canada since 1930 and, as it turned out, the

last. The body was shipped to Preston and finished off by railway forces, who also fabricated the trucks. Numbered 626, it was mostly express space and was put in service between Galt and Kitchener where it spent all its life. It was capable of running in multiple with the other cars on the line.

ABANDONMENT REJECTED

Post-war optimism did not last, however, as passenger business began to decline; the railway applied for permission to abandon all passenger services in April 1950. This was refused by the Board of Transport Commissioners after protests from the towns served, but schedules were slashed. Service on the

Cars 846 937, 848
and 864 northbound
on the Freeport bridge
May 1, 1955
on a special "post-
abandonment" excursion
(RJS)

"Hespeler Express" was cut from continuous shuttle service to 16 trips a day scheduled at odd times; Galt-Kitchener service was down to eight trips a day run largely for express traffic. Sunday service on the Hespeler branch was ended in September 1952. The final time-table (1954) showed no service at all on Sundays, and no through rail service between Galt and Kitchener on any day. This was because car 626 in itself represented the only passenger service on the G.R.R. and when it happened to reach Preston, either northbound or southbound, it hastened to Hespeler and back.

In this period, maintenance was not permitted to decline; in fact the general appearance of the property was better in 1955 than it had been in 1950. Considerable money was spent on work equipment, and both M-4 and M-6, ex-C.P.E.L. maintenance cars at the Rockwood museum, were given their present appearance during those years. A new yard and freight house were opened in September 1952 at Victoria St. in Kitchener.

PASSENGER RUNS END

A renewed application for abandonment was granted, and passenger service on both railways ended together on April 23, 1955. The last scheduled run on the Grand River Railway was by car 844 Hespeler to Preston. Excursions for railway enthusiasts were held on April 24 (five cars) and May 1 (four cars), and passenger moves were made on one or two

occasions in the next few weeks for special parties. It was found, however, that the sight of passenger cars on the line resulted in demands for restoration of service, so this procedure was soon terminated. The last recorded movement of a passenger car was a round trip Preston to Paris on August 30, 1956. There was some hope of selling the cars for further service, so they were stored at Preston and Brantford until late in 1956 when they were unceremoniously burnt out, cut up and dumped into railway freight cars for sale as scrap. Cars 622 and 626 survived until May 1957 when they met the same fate.

Electric freight operation continued, and so did surprises; in May 1958 45-ton box-cab motor 222, the oldest and lightest on the line, was rebuilt from the ground up at Preston as virtually a new 70-ton engine, entirely different in appearance. Other improvements were made at the same time as two tracks at Preston shop were "de-electrified" for use by diesel locomotives.

DIESELIZATION

The end of electric operation came on October 1, 1961 when motors 228 and 337 hauled an extra freight train from Galt to Waterloo and returned to Preston. The last electric passenger movement, a most unusual one, had been made the previous day when the same motors hauled an excursion train made up of C.P.R. coaches, from Galt interchange

Motor 222, new and old:
Upper: New 222 built at Preston in 1958 (OPM)
Below: as rebuilt in 1918 from GP&H motor 10 (OPM)
Third: Preston Shop, small but resourceful (JMM)
Bottom: There was very little street trackage. Car 953 on Caroline Street, Waterloo, on an excursion, May 1953 (RJS)

to Preston, then south to Simcoe and back to Galt. This was intended as the final act of the electrical era; the freight movement on the next day was unscheduled and was caused by a shortage of diesels.

In 1960 the City of Kitchener and the railway agreed on removal of G.R.R. track paralleling King St. between Centreville and Ottawa St. A new line, not electrified, was built from near Centreville to the disused C.N. Galt branch, which was used by G.R.R. as far as the point where the two lines came together near Queen St. These changes lengthened the G.R.R. line by less than a mile, and were completed in the summer of 1962.

The Grand River Railway retains its corporate existence and its head office at Preston, but is operated exclusively by C.P.R. diesels. Most of the former double track has been singled, Preston station has been demolished and the shop, now officially an engine terminal, was remodelled in 1969 for better storage of the diesels. Relics of its street-railway past can still be found in street trackage on freight branches in Kitchener, Waterloo and Galt, the latter being ex-Grand Valley whose "roadside-trolley" ancestry could not be more obvious.

Regular Canadian Pacific Transport bus service was taken over by Canada Coach Lines in March 1957, C.P.T. buses operating only the train-connection trips, which were in turn discontinued in 1964.

2

Lake Erie & Northern Railway

While the Grand River Railway was almost the first Canadian interurban to be built, its partner, the Lake Erie & Northern, was almost the last. It originated in 1910 as a Brantford promotion, which obtained a Dominion charter in the following year and qualified for the standard government subsidy of $6,400 per mile constructed. L.E.& N. bonds were purchased by Brantford and most of the towns along the route. Construction began in May 1913 under the guidance of W.P. Kellett, who had previously been General Manager of the neighbouring Grand Valley Railway. The original intention was to use the west bank of the river between Paris and Galt, presumably to avoid conflict with the G.V.R., but it was changed to the east bank, and the Ayr branch dropped, when the C.P.R. assumed control early in 1911.

It is a little difficult to understand the motives behind this, unless to keep the line out of the hands of a competitor; the C.P. already had a substantial foothold in the area through its half-ownership of the Toronto Hamilton & Buffalo Ry. whose line between Brantford and Waterford was within sight of the L.E.& N. route in some places. There was at this time, however, a rather surprising interest in carferry services across the Lower Lakes and it was in this era that most of them were started: those serving Port Stanley, Port Burwell and Port Maitland on Lake Erie and Cobourg on Lake Ontario. The C.P.R. certainly hoped to use Port Dover as a car-ferry terminal but the necessary harbour improvements were not made so that the L.E.& N. never developed the freight-traffic potential that the C.P.R. probably saw in it. This may have been partly the result of opposition by the Grand Trunk which handled a certain amount of coal at Port Dover, and effectively controlled the small harbour as far as railway use was concerned. The line's original promoters laid much stress on the benefits to Brantford of

a direct connection to the Ohio and Pennsylvania coal and steel regions via a car ferry, and inserted in the charter the very unusual provision that the L.E.& N. Railway, in addition to normal railroad activities, was empowered to buy and sell coal and iron.

Whatever the reason, the C.P.R. revamped the L.E.& N. project, upgrading construction standards, eliminating planned street running in Brantford and Simcoe, and integrating the management with that of the Grand River Railway. C.P.R. steam engines were used on construction trains.

ROUTE DECIDED

The route as completed began at an end-on junction with the C.P.R. "downtown freight spur" in Galt, and ran close beside the Grand River at the bottom of the broad valley, possibly the most continuously beautiful interurban section in Eastern Canada. Just north of Paris the line climbed out of the valley but followed the course of the river to Brantford. It then swung across country through prosperous farming territory via Mount Pleasant, Oakland, Waterford and Simcoe to Port Dover, a distance of 51 miles from Galt. A long high viaduct crossed over the New York Central and a small pond at Waterford.

North of Brantford the line parallelled the Grand Valley Railway. Rather than having to suffer the older line's competition, and as a means (never followed through) of providing a low-level freight spur into Paris from the north, the L.E.& N. tried to buy the G.V.R. at a bankrupt sale in 1914, but the successful purchaser was the City of Brantford. The City, however, was interested only in the street railway, and was willing to dispose of the 13 miles north of Paris for the bargain price of $30,000.

Although the affiliated Grand River

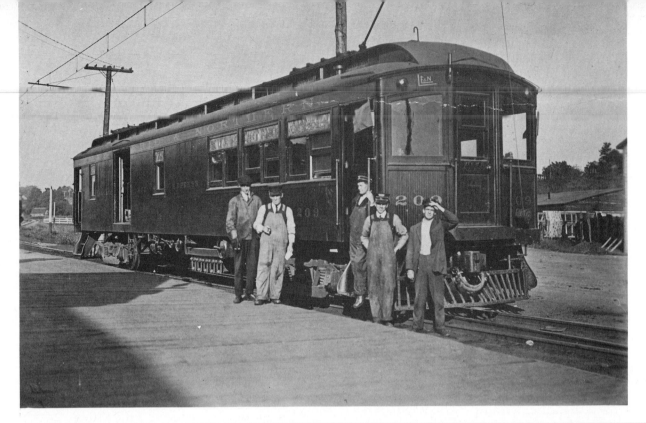

Railway was a 600-volt line, the L.E.&N. was electrified on the newer 1500-volt system which, instead of needing six substations, required only 2½ in the 51 miles, the fraction representing a boxcar-sized portable substation located temporarily at Galt and discontinued after Preston substation was opened in 1921. The other substations were in the passenger station building at Simcoe and in the Brantford carhouse.

Catenary overhead was installed in a manner very similar to that erected at the same time on the Toronto Suburban's Guelph line, and it is possible that, if the owners had not been competing railroads, some attempt might have been made to link the two lines which were separated only by a 6-mile gap between Hespeler and Guelph. (Had the Toronto Suburban's plans been completed, the lines would have connected in Kitchener.)

There were no trolley frogs at any main-line switch, in order to make the overhead readily useable by pantagraphs and to avoid high-speed dewirements with trolley poles; the poles had to be shifted from one wire to another at switches by the conductor. At car-houses and yards there were sometimes six or seven wires, one for each track, all crowded as closely as possible together over the throat of the yard.

NEW CARS

The cars were built by Preston Car & Coach Co., with Baldwin trucks built under license by Canadian Locomotive Co., Kingston. There were eight cars: four passenger motors, two passenger trailers and two express-passenger combines. Their design was characteristic of the years of transition from wood to steel construction. They were sheathed in wood, largely for the sake of insulation, but the frame was entirely of steel and there was a steel "inner skin" beneath the wooden sheathing. Other cars built at the same time (such as those on the Toronto Suburban, also built by Preston) dispensed with the exterior wood altogether, and thus had a somewhat more modern appearance. The C.P.R. influence was very obvious in the appearance of the L.E.&N. cars, which were unlike any other Canadian interurbans. They were more strongly built than the usual electric car; the framing was

Left, upper: Car 209, later 797, at the Grand Trunk (CNR) station, Port Dover, about 1918 (WEM)
Left, lower: Cars 953 and 862 southbound at Galt May 10, 1953 (RJS).
Below: 797 at Hespeler, August 1947, partly steel-sheathed (WH)
Right: interior of car 933 (RJS)

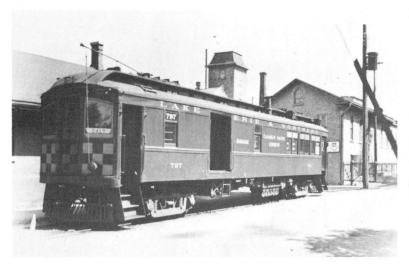

Two views of Brantford station. Above: 1920 showing two B.&H. cars ready to leave for Hamilton, (OPM). Below: Car 842 southbound loading express. (NM)

Car 255 (later 939) on Water St. at Concession St., Galt, during the first month of operation, March, 1916.
The car is leaving the former Grand Valley line northbound, joining the G.P. & H. (seen curving in from the right) on its way to the latter's station near Main St. (HEPC)

designed to withstand the stresses of locomotive haulage in trains, and extra lateral strength was provided by three horizontal stiffeners extending across the interior below the level of the clerestory roof. The result was that at 40 years of age they showed little if any structural deterioration or distortion.

The only L.E. & N. car barn was a small one at Brantford. Most cars were stored at Preston even in low-voltage years of the G.R.R.; the newer cars could run at reduced speed on 600 volts. For the first few years the actual physical connection with the G.R.R. was via the former G.V.R. line along Water St. South, and this was normally used by L.E. & N. cars to reach the G.P. & H. station. There was no L.E. & N. station at Galt in the early years.

LINE OPENS

The outbreak of war in August 1914 caused a six-month pause in the work, but construction was soon resumed and the line was completed during 1915. Grand Valley Ry. operations were abandoned north of Paris on February 3, 1916 when spring floods damaged the track. The L.E. & N. began running on February 7 between Galt and a temporary terminal near the Lorne Bridge in Brantford. This was earlier than had been planned and was scarcely a week after completion of the overhead had allowed training runs to begin; the first test run had been made with car 225 (later 933) on February 2.

Immediately north of the Lorne Bridge it was necessary to rebuild Water St. and con-

struct a massive retaining wall to protect residences on Jubilee Terrace, in order to make space for the new track in a very restricted location. The bridge itself had to be raised seven feet for proper clearance. This delayed opening the rest of the line, and it was not until June 2, 1916 that passenger service was begun between Brantford and Simcoe. South of there, service began on July 1 but was terminated after a few hours owing to power-supply troubles. A makeshift steam-operated service catered for beach excursion traffic until the electric cars started running again on July 22.

There was a delay in completion of the line to the beach caused by a dispute with the village of Port Dover which wanted the electric cars to run through the streets while the C.P. was anxious to avoid street running and the severe curvature that would be entailed. In the event, after prolonged negotiations a connection was made with the Grand Trunk and the catenary carried 0.6 miles over steam-line rails to the old G.T.R. (later Canadian National) station at the lake. Operation to this point began on July 8, 1917. There was therefore no street running whatever on the L.E. & N. main line.

Attractive station buildings were erected at Paris, Mount Pleasant, Oakland, Waterford and Simcoe, and an old stone house beside the line was adapted at Glen Morris. At Brantford a two-level station was built at the Lorne Bridge. The waiting room opened onto the bridge and the rails were directly underneath. The station was opened on March 12, 1917 and was also used by the Brantford & Hamilton Electric Railway. (until this date, an old box

Left: Motor 50, and excursion train at Port Dover, about 1919 or 1920.
Below: 624 and 848 southbound at Simcoe, October 1951. (RJS)

car parked at Scarfe Ave. served as a temporary L.E.& N. station). Through interline tickets were sold between the two lines.

Passenger traffic on the L.E.& N. was never particularly heavy and the maximum service operated was every two hours. Freight service was handled by electric motors which at first had both a pantagraph and trolley poles. (The passenger cars were strengthened for installation of pantagraphs but this was never done and those on the motors were soon removed). One of the motors had a higher top speed than the other and was designed for passenger service hauling trailers or railway coaches, but this practice ceased in the early 'twenties.

EXPRESS

Canadian Pacific express was handled in electric cars from Galt to all points on the line. In later years enough shipments moved between Galt and Brantford to occupy G.R.R. express car 622 full-time; this operated in multiple with L.E.& N. passenger cars which looked after express shipments for other points on the line by piling the packages on the front seats. G.R.R. combine 624 was also frequently used in this service. The electric lines served only as operating agents for C.P. Express, providing the cars and being paid a flat daily rate for doing so. The shipments were actually handled (except for the rather makeshift arrangement on L.E.& N. passenger cars already referred to) by C.P. Express personnel riding on the cars. It was a long-standing contention of the authorities at Preston that the financial arrangements unduly favoured the parent at the expense of the Electric Lines. Carload freight was interchanged with the C.P.R. and G.R.R. at Galt, with the N.Y.C. at Waterford and, a few years later and after a government order, with the C.N.R. at Simcoe and Brantford.

Through passenger tickets were sold to and from all points on the Canadian Pacific transportation empire, and it was possible (in theory at least) to buy tickets at a L.E.& N. station for a journey to Hong Kong or Liverpool; by rail to Vancouver, Montreal or Quebec and then one of the C.P. "Empress" liners on the high seas.

The LE&N at Main Street, Galt. Above: the new station about 1938, built just beyond the shelter visible in the above photograph (CPR). Below: 1919, before the Grand River's new line was built. The wire extended about a quarter-mile north (CPEL).

Car 846 northbound on the L.E.&N. line near Glen Morris (WCJ).

NEW CARS

Immediately after the war, as detailed elsewhere, the Grand River Railway was rebuilt, converted to 1500-volt power and re-equipped with cars that were all-steel versions of the 1915 cars and could operate in multiple with them. Two of the steel cars were lettered for the L.E.&N. but were identical with the G.R.R. cars. The C.P. "downtown spur" in Galt was transformed into the double-track main line of the new G.R.R., which now met the L.E.&N. end-on at Main St. The two formed thereafter for all practical purposes a single railroad.

The two L.E.&N. trailers were motorized and all the wooden cars were renumbered into the new numbering system whose intricacies are detailed elsewhere. The earlier dark green ("Brewster Green") uniform gave place in due course to C.P.R. maroon but otherwise the appearance of the cars changed very little throughout their long lives apart from steel exterior sheathing applied in later years to the combines. In post-war years, in an effort to

reduce grade-crossing accidents by increasing visibility, various patterns of yellow-and-black paint were applied to the car ends, which may have been startling but was definitely not handsome.

The G.R.R. gave up running on Water St. in Galt in 1921, thus isolating the West Side Freight Spur which thenceforth had to be reached by using the 3/5 mile of the former G.V.R. which had served as temporary connection for the L.E.&N. to the G.P.&H. A very short section of G.P.&H. street track was retained, thus maintaining access to the freight line.

IMPROVEMENTS

In the immediate post-war years a number of improvements were made to the L.E.& N. line, completing original plans that had not been carried out owing to war conditions. Chief among these was the opening in December 1923 of a large new station at Main St. in Galt, used by both lines. The original station at Waterford was destroyed by fire in April 1922 and rebuilt, the new structure being opened on December

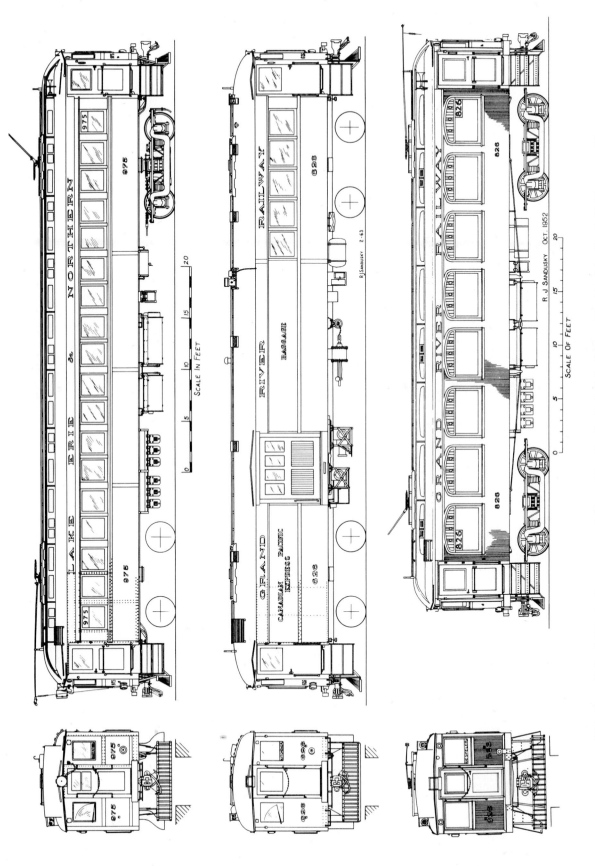

975: Two of the 1921 steel cars were lettered for the L.E.&N. but were identical to the G.R.R. cars. They were almost unchanged in appearance during their 35 years of service.
626: The last interurban car built in Canada. Normally ran north of the C.P.R. station, Galt only, and was scrapped when less than ten years old.
826: Originally G.P.&H. 205, this car was greatly rebuilt for G.R.R. 1500-volt service and ended its days normally assigned to the "Hespeler Express". (All drawings by R.J. Sandusky.)

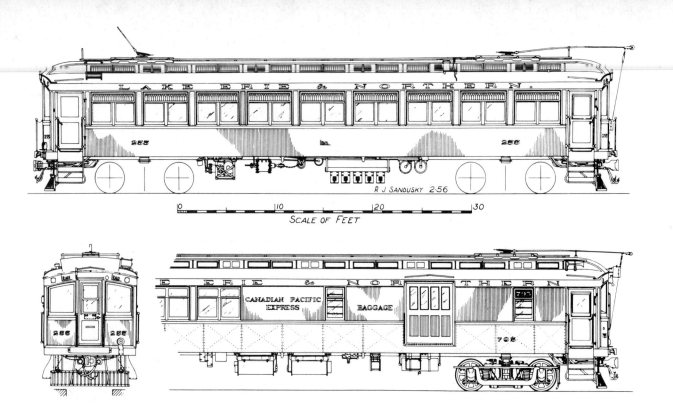

SCALE OF FEET

Above: 255, one of the wood-sheathed cars built for the opening of the L.E.&N. Line. Car 255 later was renumbered 939. (All drawings by R.J. Sandusky.)

795, one of two express-passenger combines later steel-reinforced as shown.

	STATIONS		FARE
THE GRAND RIVER RAILWAY COMPANY — Good for continuous trip only on the train and date issued and between stations punched. This is a receipt for fare paid and should be RETAINED BY PASSENGER. In case of dispute it should be sent to the General Passenger Agent, Galt, Ont., with full explanation. No stop-over allowed. M.W. KIRKWOOD, General Manager	**TO**	**FROM**	**COLLECTED**
	Galt	★	
	Golf Club	★	3
			5
	Preston	★	10
	Hagey	★	15
			20
	Freeport	★	
	Centreville	★	30
			35
	Kitchener		40
			45
	Waterloo	★	

HALF FARE

LOCAL

Nᵒ H201720 FORM 20

CONDUCTOR'S RUN	4	3	2	1
1940	1941	1942	1943	1944	1945
Jan.	Feb.	Mar.	Apl.	May	June
July	Aug.	Sept.	Oct.	Nov.	Dec.
1	2	3	4	5	6	7	8	9	10	11
12	13	14	15	16	17	18	19	20	21
22	23	24	25	26	27	28	29	30	3

1941

	STATIONS		FARE
THE GRAND RIVER RAILWAY COMPANY — Good for one continuous trip only on train and date issued and between stations punched, EXCEPT when punched "RETURN" this coupon will be good for return passage between stations punched, within one month from date punched. ___ Manager	**TO**	**FROM**	**COLLECTED**
	Hespeler	★	
	Forbes'	★	3
	Beaverdale	★	4
	Idylwild	★	5
	Speedsville	★	8
	Preston	★	10
	Pattison's	★	15
	Ea. Preston	★	

HALF FARE

RETURN

No. 582698   G.R. 21

CONDUCTOR'S RUN	4	3	2	1
1946	1947	1948	1949	1950	1951
Jan.	Feb.	Mar.	Apl.	May	June
July	Aug.	Sept.	Oct.	Nov.	Dec.
1	2	3	4	5	6	7	8	9	10	11
12	13	14	15	16	17	18	19	20	21
22	23	24	25	26	27	28	29	30	31

1947

	STATIONS		FARE
THE GRAND RIVER RAILWAY COMPANY — Good for continuous trip only on the train and between stations punched. This is a receipt for fare paid and should be RETAINED BY PASSENGER. In case of dispute it should be sent to the General Passenger Agent, Preston, Ont., with full explanation. No stop-over allowed. ___ Manager	**TO**	**FROM**	**COLLECTED**
	Galt	★	
	Whitney	★	3
	Barrett	★	5
	Preston	★	10
	Hagey	★	15
	Freeport	★	20
	Dellvue	★	25
	Centreville	★	30
	Woodlands	★	35
	Sunnyside	★	40
	Shantz	★	45
	Kitchener	★	50

HALF FARE

LOCAL

No. L753061   G.R. 20

CONDUCTOR'S RUN	4	3	2	1
1948	1949	1950	1951	1952	1953
Jan.	Feb.	Mar.	Apr.	May	June
July	Aug.	Sept.	Oct.	Nov.	Dec.
1	2	3	4	5	6	7	8	9	10	11
12	13	14	15	16	17	18	19	20	21
22	23	24	25	26	27	28	29	30	31

1949

Right: 844 and 624 southbound at Glen Morris, March 1955 (RJS)
Below: 624 and 848 at the new Port Dover station (NM)
Bottom: 848 crossing a mill pond just south of Simcoe, April 1955 (RJS)

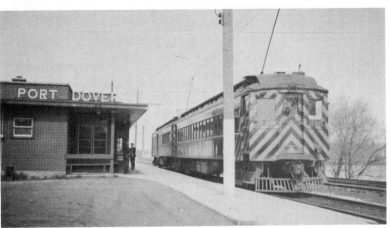

An impressive lineup at Brantford. The occasion
is unknown but was probably about 1929.
The cars are coupled in four pairs which
have been closed up for the photograph. (CPEL)

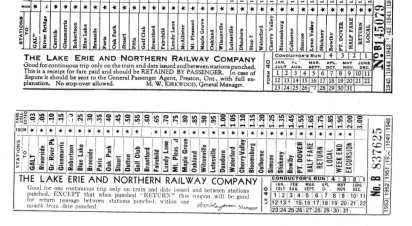

THE LAKE ERIE AND NORTHERN RAILWAY COMPANY
Good for continuous trip only on the train and date issued and between stations punched.
This is a receipt for fare paid and should be RETAINED BY PASSENGER. In case of
dispute it should be sent to the General Passenger Agent, Preston, Ont., with full explanation. No stop-over allowed.   M. W. KIRKWOOD, *General Manager.*

THE LAKE ERIE AND NORTHERN RAILWAY COMPANY
Good for one continuous trip only on train and date issued and between stations
punched, EXCEPT that when punched "RETURN" this coupon will be good
for return passage between stations punched, within one
month from date punched.   Manager

6, 1923. Fire similarly damaged the Brantford substation and carhouse in November 1920 and caused rebuilding. The fire originated in the substation, which was in the same building; while it was being rebuilt (on another site), C.P.R. 4-6-0 no. 451 was assigned to freight service on the L.E.& N. to save power.

For the next quarter century, little change occurred in L.E.& N. operations, though as detailed elsewhere, these years were eventful indeed on the Grand River. Passenger traffic reached its peak in 1921, when 609,000 were carried; ten years later this had skidded to 231,000 and it is undoubtedly owing to railroad ownership that the service was not abandoned at the time.

Following World War II, all the steel cars were modernized but the 1915 cars were untouched apart from a lighter interior paint job. Thereafter, G.R.R. cars were more often used although L.E.& N. cars continued to be in frequent demand, particularly the two combines, one of which had its passenger seats removed for additional package space. Brantford carhouse was expanded, and a new larger freight house opened there in 1946. Simcoe

service on nine trains a day over the length of the line, not notably less than the maximum of earlier days, was continued but owing to the practice of connecting with C.P. trains, an even-interval schedule was not offered. Most schedules required 1 hour 45 minutes for the 51 miles, a high average for an interurban schedule making all stops. (In addition to 14 station stops there were about 35 flag stops). C.P. Transport buses never ran south of Galt and, in fact, government regulations prevented any bus competition as long as the passenger service was provided, except for the buses which replaced Brantford's Paris suburban line in 1929.

SPARSE SERVICE

Following refusal of the first application for passenger service abandonment, L.E.& N. schedules were slashed effective August 13, 1950. Only five trains (later four) now travelled the length of the line, all connecting with C.P.R. trains. Thereafter, schedules were rather frequently altered, and it seemed to outside observers that the most efficient use was not always made of cars and crews, especially those filling additional schedules south of

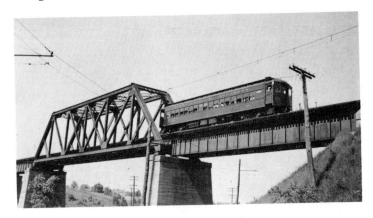 

Left: 973 on the high bridge at Waterford, June 1947 (JDK)
Right: 975 northbound at Dutton, December 1972 (RJS)

substation was re-equipped with modern electronic equipment of greater capacity replacing the original rotary machinery.

CONTRACTIONS BEGIN

In 1946 trackage rights over the C.N.R. in Port Dover were given up and a small passenger station built at Chapman St.; for a few months while it was under construction car 826 parked on a siding did duty instead. A

Brantford. This was particularly notable during the last year of passenger service when this additional car arrived at Brantford northbound at 1:50 P.M.; it remained there until 3:40 when it coupled onto the rear of a two-car southbound train from Galt. Thus it "deadheaded" to Simcoe where it uncoupled and ran north alone, leaving Simcoe at 4:30 and arriving at Brantford at 5:10. This was the end of the run, according to the public timetable, but in

Above: 939, 797 and 622 at C.P.R. station, Galt July 4, 1946 (WCJ).
Below: 973, 953 and 955 on the Grand River Railway line at Preston July 4, 1946. (WCJ).

fact the car continued north to Preston to end its day's work. Thus a single Simcoe-Brantford trip was the only revenue service performed by this car after 1:50 P.M., and it seemed almost unnecessary since the train from which it had uncoupled, after making the 7-mile run to Port Dover and back, then followed it north over the same line only 35 minutes later. Some observers saw in all this an attempt to increase operating costs in order to make a better case for passenger abandonment.

Another very strange situation at this time concerned the L.E.&N. schedule as printed in the Canadian Pacific's own timetable folder, which had always given the times at Main St. station. This was misleading since, as already mentioned, L.E.&N. cars afforded direct connections at the C.P. station, and the G.R.R. schedules in the same folder did in fact show the C.P. station times. However, in September 1953 the following special note added: "L.E.&N. trains operate to and from Main St. Station, Galt. Distance to C.P.R. Depot 3/4 of a mile. Necessary that passengers make their own arrangements for transfer between stations." This is incomprehensible since L.E.&N. cars continued to make the same connections at the C.P. station that they always had done, and carried passengers as before. It certainly did not tend to increase the number of passengers on L.E.&N. cars, and seems even more surprising in view of the fact that the very next C.P. timetable issued (April 1954) showed the C.P. station times, rather than Main St. times, for the first time.

 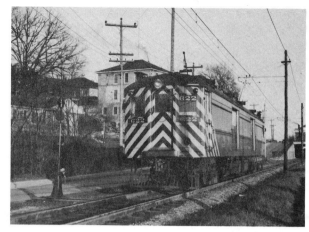

Left: 975, 624, 864 at Mt. Pleasant, last day of service, April 23, 1955. This 3-car train is referred to in the text. (RJS). Right: 622 northbound at Brantford, March, 1955. (RJS)

PASSENGER RUNS END

Passenger traffic fell to only 160,000 in 1954, and a second application for passenger abandonment was granted. Service therefore ceased on April 23, 1955, the last scheduled L.E.&N. car being 975 Galt to Port Dover and return.

The Chicago South Shore & South Bend Railroad expressed interest in some of the cars for Chicago commuter service, but test runs made on August 30, 1956 with car 864 revealed that the top speed was rather low for the South Shore Line. A bid was submitted but was rejected by the C.P.R. as being too low.

After this time, little freight service was given south of Simcoe, territory which was better served by the C.N.R., and this section was abandoned in November 1962. L.E.&N. trains began using Toronto Hamilton & Buffalo rails between Brantford and Waterford in December 1965, but the L.E.&N. was left intact though unused. Simcoe, Waterford and Paris stations were closed in 1969. Brantford "Union Station" was demolished in 1958. Electric operation ended with the excursion train of September 30, 1961 described in the G.R.R. section, by which time the maintenance of track, formerly absolutely first-class, was such as to require a severe speed limit and to cause great unhappiness among those who remembered the Lake Erie & Northern as one of the speediest and most impressive electric interurban lines.

SUMMARY

The available figures published in Government reports for the C.P. Electric Lines are rather unsatisfactory for purposes of this work. Figures are available for the G.P.&H. and G.R.R. from 1900 and for the L.E.&N. from 1917. However the two lines were combined for statistical purposes in 1932, and after 1955 were included in the overall C.P.R. figures from which they cannot be extracted. It should also be noted that, unlike Canadian National practice in the case of the Niagara St. Catharines & Toronto, highway operations of C.P. Transport were not included in the Electric Lines accounts.

The G.P.&H. and G.R.R. figures show

The last excursion train, September 30, 1961 on the Waterford viaduct. (JDK)

the expected pattern of comfortable profitability until the 'twenties, but unlike most other inter-urbans, both passenger and freight traffic held up fairly well during the decade and indeed this was probably the most profitable of Canadian interurbans at that time. Passenger loads in the first report (year ending June 30, 1900) were 228,000; this increased to 600,000 in 1907 and one million in 1911. The peak was almost exactly 1½ million in 1920, following which there was a steady decline to 743,000 in 1931, the last year of separate accounting.

Freight traffic in the first year was 17,100 tons, increasing to 44,000 in 1905, 92,100 in 1908 and 132,000 in 1910. After a peak of 203,000 in 1913, it oscillated to 139,000 in 1915, 177,000 in 1918, 140,000 in 1920 and then began a climb that took it to a pre-Depression peak of 225,000 in 1929. It had fallen to 170,000 in 1931.

The L.E.& N. was both less busy and less profitable; while it suffered an operating deficit (of exactly $3.00) only in 1931 before separate accounting ceased, it never covered all its fixed charges because of the high invest-ment resulting from its late construction date. Passenger traffic began at 373,000 in the first year, increased steadily to a peak of 609,000 in 1921, then fell equally steadily to 350,000 in 1929, dropping to 231,000 in 1931. Freight traffic was sparse, considering the 51-mile length of the line; it rose from 56,000 tons to a peak of 214,000 in 1931.

The combined railways never covered their costs after 1931, but were kept going because of their value as feeders to the parent railway. Of the 24 years for which figures are available, out-of-pocket operating losses were suffered in 14 of them, and were continuous after 1946 except for a modest surplus in the single year 1952.

In the first year of combined accounting, 839,000 passengers were handled by rail on the two lines; this fell to a low of 748,000 in 1938, climbed to 841,000 in 1940 then soared to a wartime peak of 1,680,000 in 1944. It dropped to 941,000 in 1948, 581,000 in 1950 when the first abandonment application was made; to 283,000 in 1952, and 161,000 in 1954, the last full year.

Freight operation of the combined rail-ways showed quite a different picture. Starting from 285,000 tons in 1932, tonnage actually increased during most of the Depression, reaching 389,000 tons in 1937. A slight setback was wiped out by 1940 when 388,000 tons were carried. The wartime years were unusual, since instead of a peak followed by an imme-diate decline, tonnage increased steadily through the war and kept on doing so in the postwar years: 538,000 tons in 1942, 577,000 tons in 1945, 710,000 tons in 1947 and 946,000 tons in 1951. A decline reduced tonnage to 732,000 in 1954 but this dramatically increased to 942,000 in the following year, the last for which figures are available. One wishes that a few more years' results could be tabulated, in order to follow this interesting trend.

(Note: In 1917 the town of Berlin changed its name to Kitchener, and in 1973 the towns of Galt, Preston and Hespeler were amalgamated into a single municipality called "Cambridge".)

Motor 226 and a short train northbound at Simcoe,
June, 1951. (RJS)

Lake Erie and Northern Railway   Time Table No. 1

PORT DOVER to GALT
READ UP
NORTHBOUND TRAINS—INFERIOR DIRECTION
FIRST-CLASS

Effective 12.01 a.m. May 22, 1921

GALT to PORT DOVER
READ DOWN
SOUTHBOUND TRAINS—SUPERIOR DIRECTION
FIRST-CLASS

505 a.m.	515 a.m.	255 a.m. Exp.	525 a.m.	535 p.m.	545 p.m.	265 p.m. Exp.	555 p.m.	565 p.m.	575 p.m.	Miles from Galt	Tel. phone office	STATIONS	Tel. phone Calls	570 p.m.	560 p.m.	550 p.m.	540 p.m.	530 p.m.	250 p.m. Exp.	520 a.m.	510 a.m.	240 a.m. Exp.	500 a.m.
Gn 108 s 8.42		Gn 120 s 11.42		Gn 132 s 2.45	s 4.45	s 5.30 GR 46				.64	T	C. P. R. Junction, Galt		s 6.45	s 4.45	s 2.45		s 12.20		s 8.45	Gn 109 s 7.05		
s 8.39	s 10.43	s 11.40	12.13	2.43	4.43	s 5.25	s 6.43	8.43	11.01	.00	T	Main St., Galt		s 9.15	s 6.55	s 4.55	s 2.55	12.50	s 12.25	s 10.50	s 8.55	s 7.08	6.55
f 8.37	f 10.40	f 11.39	12.10	2.40	4.40	f 5.23	f 6.40	8.40	11.02	.37		xConcession St., Galt		f 9.18	f 6.57	f 4.57	f 2.57	12.52	f 12.27	f 10.52	8.57		6.57
f 8.35	f 10.38	f 11.37	12.38	2.38	4.38	f 5.21	f 6.38	8.38	11.00	1.07	T	Soap Works		f 9.20	f 6.59	f 4.59	f 2.59	12.54	12.38	f 10.54	f 8.59	f 7.12	6.59
f			250							2.06		xMcPherson		f					525				
f										2.15		xRiver Bridge		f									
f										4.47		xCarrick		f									
f										5.03		xMcRae		f		265							
s 8.25	s 10.29	s 11.27	s 12.29	2.29	4.29	s 5.09	s 6.29	8.29	10.51	6.73	D T	Glen Morris		s 9.30	s 7.09	s 5.09	3.09	1.04	12.48	s 11.04	s 9.09	s 7.22	7.10
f			550							9.38		xRobertson		f									
f										10.85		xBlue Lake		f									
f										11.64		xBraeside		f					255				
s 8.12	s 10.15	s 11.17	s 12.15	2.15	4.15	s 4.55	s 6.15	8.15	10.40	13.32	D T	Paris		s 9.43	s 7.22	s 5.22	s 3.22	1.17	1.05	s 11.17	s 9.22	s 7.40	7.23
f		520	pm							15.21		xOak Park		f									
f										16.47		xStuart		f									
f										17.80		xHardy		f									
f 240										18.62		xGolf Club		f									
500—									570	20.30		xWest Mill St., Brantford		f									
7.55	10.00	10.55	12.00	2.00	4.00	4.35	6.00	8.00	10.25	21.10	D T	Brantford K	B F	s 10.00	s 7.37	s 5.37	s 3.37	1.34	1.20	s 11.34	s 9.37	s 7.55	7.38
s 7.43	s 9.55	s 10.40	s 11.55	1.55	3.55	s 4.18	s 5.55	s 7.55	s 9.55	22.17	L	xMt. Pleasant Road	575	10.25	7.42	5.42	3.42	1.42	1.30	11.42	s 9.42	505 s 8.20	505 7.45
f 7.36	f 9.49	f 10.34	f 11.49	1.49	3.49	f 4.13	s 5.49	f 7.49	f 9.49	23.70	T	Fairchild		f 10.31	f 7.49	f 5.49	f 3.49	1.49	1.36	f 11.49	f 9.49	f 8.26	7.51
f		510	520	530	540		550	560		25.10		xLundy Lane	5 65	555	545	535			525	515			
f										25.70		xMcAlister					535						
s 7.30	s 9.43	s 10.28	s 11.43	1.43	3.43	s 4.07	s 5.43	s 7.43	s 9.43	26.17	D T	Mt. Pleasant		s 10.37	s 7.55	s 5.55	s 3.55	1.55	1.43	s 11.55	s 9.55	s 8.32	7.57
f		250				540				27.73		xMaple Grove		f					pm				
s 7.24	s 9.37	s 10.22	s 11.37	1.37	3.37	s 4.01	s 5.37	s 7.37	s 9.37	29.45	T	Oakland		s 10.43	s 8.01	s 6.01	s 4.01	2.01	1.48	s 12.01	s 10.01	s 8.37	8.03
f										32.10		xWilsonville		f			265						
f										33.78		xLutesville		f							255		
f 7.11	f 9.24	f 10.11	f 11.24	1.24	f 3.24	f 3.45	s 5.24	f 7.24	f 9.24	34.41	T	Dundurn		f 10.53	f 8.11	f 6.11	f 4.11	2.11	1.58	f 12.11	f 10.11	f 8.46	8.14
f		510								35.70		xStop No. 7		f									
										36.50		Bunker Hill											
s 7.08	s 9.21	s 10.08	s 11.21	1.21	s 3.21	s 3.40	s 5.21	s 7.21	s 9.21	36.72	T	Waterford		s 10.56	s 8.15	s 6.15	s 4.15	2.15	2.05	s 12.15	s 10.15	s 8.50	8.18
										38.26		Cherry Valley											
										40.20		xBloomsburg											
		240								42.09		xColborne									515		
s 6.55	s 9.07	s 9.55	s 11.07	1.07	3.07	s 3.25	s 5.07	s 7.07	9.07	43.62	D T	Simcoe	S O	s 11.08	s 8.27	s 6.27	s 4.27	2.27	2.20	s 12.27	s 10.27	s 9.07	8.30
										45.51		xLynn Valley											
										46.64		xStickney											
										48.00		xBowlby											
f 6.43	f 8.54	f 9.39	f 10.54	12.54	2.54	3.08	f 4.54	f 6.54	8.54	50.00		Main St. Pt. Dover		f 11.18	f 8.39	f 6.39	f 4.39	2.39	2.30	f 12.39	f 10.39	f 9.19	8.42
												Staff System Absolute											
f 6.42	f 8.53	f 9.38	f 10.53	12.53	f 2.53	3.07	4.53	6.53	8.53	50.40	T	xIvey's Jct.		f 11.19	f 8.40	f 6.40	f 4.40	2.40	2.31	f 12.40	10.40	f 9.20	8.43
												to											
s 6.40	s 8.50	s 9.35	s 10.50	12.50	s 2.50	3.05	s 4.50	s 6.50	8.50	51.00	D T	Pt. Dover K		s 11.22	s 8.43	s 6.43	s 4.43	2.43	2.35	s 12.43	s 10.43	s 9.23	8.45

"•" Daily.
"†" Daily except Sunday.
"*" No passing track.
"S" Regular stop.
"F" Flag stop to receive or discharge passengers or freight.
"L" Leave.
"A" Arrive.
"DT" Day telephone or telegraph station.
"NT" Night telephone or telegraph station.
"T" Telephone station.
"K" Comparison clock, registering and bulletin point.
"B" Bulletin Point.
"X" No passing track.
"Q" Cross over.

L. E. & N. Ry. Trains 505, 255, 535, 545, 265, are timed at C. P. R. Jct. Galt on G. R. Ry., and will run over G. R. Ry. tracks between Main St. Galt, and C. P. R. Jct., Galt, and meet G.R. Ry. trains as indicated on the time table.

SPECIAL INSTRUCTIONS

Main line is from C. P. R. freight shed, Main Street, Galt, to Ivey's Mileage 50.4, Port Dover. Normal position of switches must be for main line.

Main track switches must be locked and other switches secured. After a switch is turned, the points must be examined to know that they are in proper position.

Bulletin Points: Preston Junction, Brantford, Brantford and Port Dover and Port Dover passenger station.

Timetable: Heavy faced figures denote meeting points of opposing trains. Small figures placed above heavy faced figures denote the number of opposing trains.

Where one time is given for a station it is the leaving time; where two, they are the arriving and leaving time.

RAILWAY CROSSINGS AT GRADE.

With Grand Trunk Railway at Mileage .74. Interlocked and derails in both lines. Normal position of signals Stop. Trains must not pass home signals until clear indication is given.

With Brantford Municipal Railway, West Mill Street, Mileage 20.30. Not interlocked. Train order signal on L. E. & N. only. Not yet in operation. All trains must STOP 200 feet from diamond crossing and movement over this crossing must be preceded by a flag man, and track known to be clear before signal to proceed is given.

With Grand Trunk Railway at Mileage 21.20. Interlocked and derails in both lines.

With T. H. & B. Ry. at Mileage 21.25. Interlocked and derails in both lines.

With Grand Trunk Railway at Mileage 44.34. Interlocked and derails in both lines.

South bound trains must stop north of Concession St., Galt.

South bound trains must not exceed a speed of ten (10) miles per hour over the road crossing in the Paris Yard, south of the G. T. R. Subway.

Trains North or South bound must not exceed a speed of ten (10) miles per hour over Victoria St., Simcoe.

Trains North or South bound must not exceed a speed of ten (10) miles per hour over Bowlby Road Crossing. Mileage 48.00.

Trains must not exceed a speed of ten (10) miles per hour over joint section with G. T. Railway between Ivey's Jct. and Port Dover.

Galt Yard Limits.
From Hunter's Corners, Galt, on G. R. Railway to yard limit board located 40 rods south of switch at Soap Works, on L.E. & N. Ry., Mileage 1.07.

Paris Yard Limits.
From yard limit board located 40 rods north of North Switch to passing track and yard limit board located 40 rods south of Gravel Pit switch.

Brantford Yard Limits.
From yard limit board located 40 rods north of switch leading to T. C. Johnson & Sons, private siding north of Morrell St. to south end of bridge over Grand River.

Between West Mill St. and T. H. & B. Ry. Diamond, Motorman will run on series only.

Waterford Yard Limits.
From yard limit board located 40 rods north of North Switch to passing track Bunker Hill to yard limit board located 40 rods south of switch to M. C. R. interchange.

Trains will use through siding north of Bunker Hill to meet and pass.

Simcoe Yard Limits.
From yard limit board located 40 rods north of shed track switch to north distant signal north of G. T. Ry. crossing south of Simcoe.

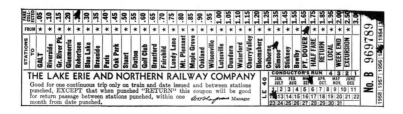

3

Brantford Street Railway
Brantford Municipal Railway

The Brantford Street Railway was incorporated by local interests in 1879 but nothing happened until March 1886 when the franchise was sold to C.H. Flack of Cornwall, Ont. who organized a new company under the old name. Construction began on July 7 of that year and proceeded rapidly so that opening ceremonies were held only two months later, on September 9, 1886. Free rides were available for all, and while the cars derailed "rather frequently", they were light in weight and easily manhandled back on the tracks.

Stables and car sheds were at Gilkison and Oxford (now West Colborne) streets, and rails were laid on three routes: to the G.T.R. station on Colborne St. at Clarence (later extended to Park Ave.), to the G.T.R. main line station out Market St., and via King, Darling, William, Richmond and Brant Ave., to the School for the Blind. Gauge was 3'6", and 5 miles of flat iron rail was in operation within two years, using three open and four closed cars. The latter were named: C.B. Boyd (named for the Mayor), R. Henry, S.G. Read and A. Harris (the last three were named for prominent local citizens.

The tracks had evidently been hastily and inefficiently built, and derailments were so frequent that newspapers eventually made mention of the fact that "yesterday not one of the street cars left the tracks." The paving materials used were too soft, and the horses gradually wore a deep trough mid-way between the rails, to the detriment of other users of the street.

This scene is believed to be on Brant Ave. about 1890. (OPM)

ELECTRIFICATION

Late in 1892 a second new company was organized, still with the same name. It ordered six new electric cars from Patterson & Corbin, St. Catharines, and rebuilt the tracks to standard gauge. In the rebuilding process, the circuitous William St. routing was abandoned in favour of a line straight out Brant Ave. Thus was formed the system's most important route, identified throughout the life of the street railway simply as "Main Line". Electric operation began on March 31, 1893. The Vice-President of the company was Samuel Insull (then described as "Second Vice-President of the Edison Electric Co.") so that the Brantford St. Ry. might be thought of as a very early component of the Insull utilities empire.

A new carhouse and power station were built on Colborne St. near the G.T.R. Tillsonburg branch crossing (often referred to as the Great Western station), and two large loop lines were constructed. The first (1893) was the East Ward loop on which cars ran via Park Ave., Arthur, Brock, Nelson and Alfred to Colborne. (In 1909 the track on Park Ave. was replaced by a new line on Alfred St.) In the following year, a second loop was created by construction of tracks from the G.T.R. main line station on Market St. via West, Duke and Palace Sts. to Brant Ave. This was evidently found too ambitious as the rails were removed later in the same year, the date of abandonment being October 22. Market St. thus resumed its former status of being a stub-end shuttle service, which it remained. Also in 1894, the Eagle Place line was built via South Market St. and Erie Ave. to Cayuga.

In 1895 a 42-acre tract called Mohawk Park (formerly Lovejoy's Grove) was leased just east of the city, and the street railway extended their line into the park. At this time the company operated $8\frac{1}{2}$ miles of track; new construction used 60-lb. rail but evidently the 30-lb. horse-car rail was still in use on some of the older sections. Twelve cars were owned (unfortunately data is lacking), and about this time the company enclosed the front platforms as protection for the motormen.

The company was not prosperous, and was unable to keep up payments on a $125,000 mortgage to Canadian General Electric Co. in connection with electrification. The mortgage was foreclosed in 1897, and C.G.E. became owner of the line, installing its President, Frederick Nicholls, as President of the B.S.R. (This debt was always a source of difficulty to the company until paid off by the city about 1936.)

Above: cars 1, 2 and 3 on Colborne St. near Clarence, 1893. (OPM) Below: car 8 on Brant Ave. at St. Paul's Ave., about 1902. (OPM)

ENTER ICKES

About this time there appears on the scene a nebulous company and a "fast operator", in particular the Von Echa Company and Dr. S. Ritter Ickes. Much mystery surrounds the Von Echa Co.; it was incorporated in West Virginia in 1900 primarily for mining enterprises, but it possessed wide powers according to its charter.

Just how Ickes became interested in

Ontario electric lines is not known. He first appeared as contractor on the Woodstock Thames Valley & Ingersoll, which he saw as a segment of a Hamilton-London interurban. The B.S.R. fitted into these plans so, in the name of the Von Echa Co., he acquired the line in July 1902 from C.G.E. which accepted $120,000 in bonds as payment. For purposes of operation, he merged the B.S.R. with the Port Dover, Brantford, Berlin & Goderich, a railway company which he controlled but whose only asset thus far was a charter. The combined company was then renamed Grand Valley Railway. Corporate amalgamation of the two companies did not come until 1907.

A 50-year franchise was obtained from the City of Brantford (effective June 18, 1902) which exempted the company from all payments to the municipality for the first 25 years. Ickes proceeded to build an interurban line to Paris, rebuilt some of the cars and extended the power house. A minor track extension was made on Brant Ave. from Palmerston to St. Paul, and the track on Palmerston between Brant Ave. and St. Paul was removed. The franchise provided that service frequency was to increase as population grew, reaching every 10 minutes when the city had 30,000 inhabitants.

EXIT ICKES

In 1905, however, Ickes disappeared as suddenly as he had appeared; bills went unpaid and creditors pressed. His whereabouts were unknown for a time, until word was received that he had died in April 1906 in Seattle, Wash., leaving behind a tangle of legal and financial problems. The Von Echa Company sold its railway assets and in May 1906 a government investigator reported that the company "was practically out of business, that Ickes was practically the company, and that other shareholders were purely nominal." Whether Ickes in fact absconded with company funds is uncertain; this was one of the allegations made when the company was wound up in 1909, but

so far as is known was never proved one way or the other.

The purchaser of the system (November 1905) was a Toronto group headed by A.J. Pattison, which retained control only briefly, selling out after two years to M.A. Vernor of Pittsburgh. The new owners formally amalgamated the B.S.R., the G.V.R. and the Woodstock Thames Valley & Ingersoll under the G.V.R. name, but to ensure continuity, only the story of the Brantford city lines will be continued in this section.

One peculiarity of Ickes management was that the cars received names rather than numbers. Those that had been numbered and subsequently named, when again numbered received different numbers from those they had borne originally, and no written record of these transformations has been preserved. This, coupled with the extensive rebuilding programme going on at the time, has rendered preparation of an accurate equipment list impossible.

The Vernor management wished to alter certain franchise terms, and the City took the opportunity of demanding substantial improvements and extensions, exacting a cash bond from the company as surety for their being made. There then ensued seven years of constant friction between the company and the city, the details of which would be too tedious to explore. The truth was that the Paris-Galt interurban extension built in 1904 was losing

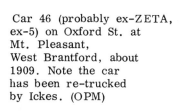

Car 46 (probably ex-ZETA,
ex-5) on Oxford St. at
Mt. Pleasant,
West Brantford, about
1909. Note the car
has been re-trucked
by Ickes. (OPM)

money heavily and the company was unable or unwilling to make many of the improvements demanded.

On May 6, 1905 the company abandoned two blocks of track at the outer end of Oxford Street. In March 1908 the Brantford generating plant was closed down and power for operation there was purchased from the Western Counties Electric Co., a subsidiary of Dominion Power & Transmission Co. of Hamilton. In 1909 yet another change of ownership occurred; the new interests were Toronto men headed by G.B. Woods. It may be that this step represents a sort of co-operative investment by the Woods and Vernor groups, as active management continued to be in the hands of the Vernor family.

SOME IMPROVEMENT

The new company at first tried to improve matters. Brant, Colborne and Market Sts. were relaid with 80-lb. rail and partly double-tracked, and a "grand union" made in England was optimistically installed at Colborne & Market Sts. The Holmedale line was built and partially opened on July 25, 1911, and completed on August of the same year. Other extensions were called for in the franchise, and the track connections for them were installed in existing lines as part of the rehabilitation work. Most of them were never built, and the useless curves and switches were removed in the 'twenties.

Service on the Eagle Place line was suspended for over a year while a new bridge was built over the canal, and was resumed on December 6, 1911 through-routed with Holmedale. Bridge trouble continued, when in January 1912 the Lorne Bridge, an old structure built before the days of electric cars, was condemned forcing suspension of the West Brantford line. Trackage on the East Ward loop was rehabilitated in 1912, as was Erie Ave. in the following year, though new rail was not laid at this time.

In May 1912 the company went into receivership, and two years later, with the interurban line in such bad condition that its operation was held to be unsafe, certain bond-holders sued the Directors for misuse of funds, and the City began action to cancel the franchise for non-performance by the company of its obligations thereunder, and for unpaid taxes. The railway was put up for sale, and the higher of the two bids received was from the city; the other being from the Lake Erie & Northern. The terms of purchase were overwhelmingly approved at a plebescite in March 1914 (1317 votes to 83) and the City assumed ownership of the system on August 5, 1914 for $253,000, plus assumption of liabilities under the C.G.E. mortgage. Ceremonies marking municipal control were not held until December 17 so that the first of the new cars ordered by the City could take part.

MUNICIPAL OWNERSHIP

The City proceeded to make a number of improvements in both local and interurban

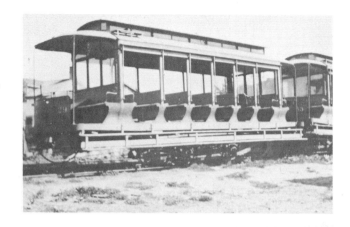

Open car 29 after retirement,
June 1910 (OPM)

lines. Tracks were rebuilt and old cars re-modelled. Rails were restored to Palmerston Ave., between St. Paul and Brant Ave. (once existing but removed in 1902) in order to form a loop for Main Line cars; this was opened on November 27, 1914. Mohawk Park, formerly leased, was purchased outright. Nine new cars and a snow sweeper were built, travelling from the Preston Car plant to Brantford under their own power. (The passenger cars were virtually identical with car 55 in the O.E.R.H.A. Rockwood museum collection, being built by the same firm at the same time, except that some of the Brantford cars were single-end). The new cars provided base service on all lines except Eagle Place where the track was not brought up to the required standard until 1915 when it was converted into a large loop. The two large G.V.R. open cars (80 and 82) were given air brakes, probably at the instigation of regulatory authorities following the Queenston disaster, and one side was blocked off owing to the danger of off-side boarding on the new double tracks.

In 1916 a model-T bus began running in the Terrace Hill section of the city. This was apparently unsatisfactory, so in the following year the bus was transferred to West Brantford which had seen no service at all for five years. The old rails were now removed here and eventually (in 1921) new ones were laid but unused pending completion of a new bridge. A second bus was obtained in 1920 and the two served until the resumption of streetcar service in 1924, following which they were disposed of. About this time a new pavement was laid on West Mill St. and the Holmedale line was relaid with 115-lb. rail, surprisingly heavy for the type of service operated.

Car 124, one of the first of the new cars, photographed at the car-house when quite new. Note inward-folding rear entrance doors; both leaves fold toward the right. This was a Preston characteristic shared with car 55 at the Rockwood railway museum. (OPM)

In 1910 the Grand Valley Railway was wound up and operations continued under the Brantford Municipal name. The first section of the Morrell St. line (from Grand River Ave. to the L. E. & N. crossing) was opened on December 2, 1916 and operated as part of the Holmedale line. With the abandonment of G.V.R. service north of Paris on February 2 of that year, the remaining suburban line was integrated with the city system. Two new interurban cars were purchased for it, replacing the ancient elevated-railway cars used since 1905, although one of them was retained for use when either of the new cars was not available.

The long Terrace Hill line was opened early in October, 1919. It is difficult to understand the reasoning which led to the construction of such a long belt line around the edge of the city, and indeed there was considerable dispute over its routing at the time. It does not appear to integrate well with the existing route pattern, nor did it take most passengers where they wanted to go except by very indirect means. At first it ran only to Dundas & St. Paul, but two years later when a subway was opened under the Grand Trunk it was extended south to connect with the stub built in 1916 on

Above: Two 2-car trains bound for Mohawk Park, on Colborne St. at Market about 1900 (OPM).

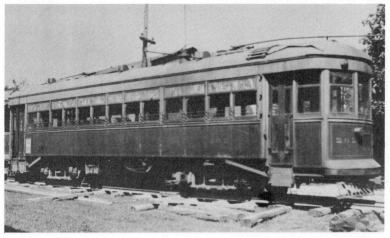

Car 202, one of two built in 1919 for the Paris line.
Except for the square upper sash, these were close to standard "Prairie Type" cars, the last ones to be built. (OPM)

Morrell St. and thereafter the Terrace Hill and Holmedale lines were operated together.

Two new cars, similar to the earlier ones, were built by Preston in 1919 and additional cars obtained second-hand: two one-man cars (the first in the city) from Pascagoula, Miss. through a second-hand equipment dealer in 1920; two from Toronto for the West Brantford line in 1923, and two Birneys from Lock Haven, Pa. in 1929. The latter were the only all-steel cars, and the only single-truck cars with air brakes. The first general use of one-man cars was on July 10, 1922 on Terrace Hill and Eagle Place lines.

MORE PROBLEMS

The city's improvements were partly at least justified by increases in the number of passengers carried (in 1916, 1,420,000; in 1919, 2,150,000) but the system as a whole continued to lose money, and in 1924 an engineering consultant was retained to survey the situation. He found that the management had been over-optimistic in its extension plans. He stated that the cars were in fair condition but needed paint and new seats. The track was good except for the Paris line which he recommended should be abandoned; he also suggested that service to Mohawk Park should be given only on weekends and holidays.

The Paris line was not immediately abandoned, but fares were increased; however it was abandoned five years later. Most of his other recommendations were not carried out. Following the Paris abandonment, limited operation continued as far as the Ava Golf Club (near old Grand Valley Park) using the two interurban cars for three months until the two Birney cars replaced them. On May 9, 1930 this service was cut back to the Brantford Golf and Country Club, and in November of that year to St. Paul Ave. The two Birney cars which had been purchased for the Mohawk Park-Ava Club service were then transferred to join the ex-Toronto cars on a new Echo Place-West Brantford route; this in turn was abandoned in 1937 and the Birney cars retired.

1: 130 as a 1-man car, 1940; half of rear door unused. 2: 131 as 1-man car, 1937; rear door eliminated. 3: 133, ex-Toronto, in 1937. 4: 135, ex-Pascagoula, in 1937. (all OPM)

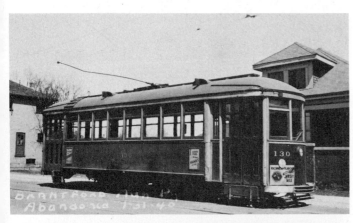

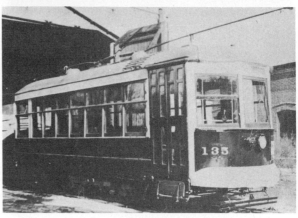

Left: Colborne Street at Market, 1928, with car 204 en route to Paris. BMRys. ticket office on right (OPM)

Below: Sweeper 50 at work on Market Street, January 1938 (OPM)

Market St. at Colborne, looking west, 1928. Cars 131 and 132 pass on Market Street. (OPM)

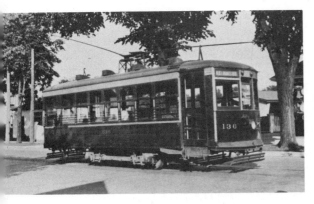

Left: Birney 136, ex-Lock Haven, in July 1935. Right: the carhouse in April 1939:
Car 128 ready for service and car 134 in course of scrapping. (OPM)

BUSES COME AND GO -
- AND COME AGAIN

In 1932 a curious development saw the creation of a new company, Mohawk Coach Lines, which with 16 buses rented from Highway King Coach Lines (which owned the company) replaced all street cars for a trial period beginning on October 1, 1932. On December 5 at the municipal elections the voters decided not to grant a franchise to Mohawk, so the street cars went back to work on January 9, 1933 and the buses were sent back to Hamilton. This adverse vote was probably at least partly the result of the motley collection of cast-off buses provided.

In 1935 the Brantford Municipal Railway name was replaced by Brantford Public Utility Commission as the railway and the local hydro distribution system were amalgamated.

Contractions began in 1935 when the Echo Place line was cut back to the end of double track (Stanley St. at the city limit). Occasional service continued beyond, to Mohawk Park. On August 23, 1937 the West Brantford line was abandoned, and in that year tracks to Mohawk Park were removed beyond Stanley St. This was the first actual track removal. On December 6, 1937 the voters decided to abandon the street railway, but by a surprisingly small majority (5718 to 4238). However, this was disallowed as, being a measure involving city investment, only ratepayers should have been permitted to vote. In a subsequent revote five months later, the ratepayers refused to auth-

orize purchase of buses, but nevertheless abandonments continued. Eagle Place and Market St. were discontinued on November 3, 1938, and on December 30, 1939 the long Terrace Hill line was abandoned. The remaining lines, the Main Line and Holmedale, ran as a single route for a few weeks until the last car was operated late on January 31, 1940; this was No. 126 which entered the carhouse at 11:45 P.M.

The carhouse was used by the buses for many years, and was finally demolished late in 1971. This building had been built in 1902 by the Grand Valley and ultimately replaced both the original B.S.R. barn and the 1893 structure on Colborne St. near Clarence. It is interesting to note that the horse-car barn at West Colborne & Gilkison Sts. was not demolished until 1937, being latterly used by the City Works Department. The Clarence St. building was built as both carhouse and generating station. In 1915 it was partially used as a station for Galt interurbans, its generating duties having been taken over by the Hydro; however it was little used as a station as a waiting room was erected at Colborne & Market Sts. in 1916. It was also used as an interurban freight station as long as such service was operated.

Much of the street railway trackage was removed in 1940 and the remainder in 1942, except for rails laid in concrete which were left in place and paved over.

The indebtedness incurred by the city in purchasing the transport system in 1914 was finally paid off in 1952.

Grand Valley Railway

The Paris line was built by the Von Echa Company under the charter rights of the Port Dover Brantford Berlin & Goderich Railway. The interurban company was legally separate from the street railway but shared common ownership and management after 1902. The Paris line was opened for traffic in March 1903 (some reports give a date of May 12, 1903) and Sunday service began on May 22, 1904.

Two handsome interurbans were built by the Ottawa Car Co. and named "Hiawatha" and "Red Cloud" as the Von Echa Co. disdained mere numbers for their cars. They turned out to use too much power for the existing generating plant, so they were returned to the builder and resold to the Toronto & York Radial Railways where they ran on the Lake Simcoe Line until 1930. They were replaced by former elevated-railway trailers from New York, rebuilt and motorized in Brantford.

Construction began in the summer of 1903 on the 13-mile Galt line that was to be the downfall of the company. Service began to a point near Blue Lake in September 1904 and and to within half a mile of Galt on November 15 of that year. The first car over the new

line was the large open car "Tuscarora"; public operation began two days later. A mail contract was held for the village of Glen Morris.

The citizens of Galt were then much in favour of strict observance of the Sabbath, and prolonged franchise negotiations centred around the question of Sunday operation of the cars. A stage coach conveyed passengers over the railless gap into Galt until agreement was reached and the line extended along Water St. to a connection with the Galt Preston & Hespeler at Concession St. Through operation began at last on October 12, 1905 with G.V.R. cars using G.P.& H. rails to reach the latter's station north of Main St. Neither line could run on Galt streets on Sundays, and G.V. cars had to terminate at the south town limits on Sundays until June 1913.

BRANCH LINE PLANNED

In 1904 a start was made on a 5 3/4 mile branch from Blue Lake to St. George. Most of the grading was eventually done, but rails were laid only 2.2 miles to the Grand Trunk Railway where an interchange was located to handle shipments of coal for the power

Left: "Hiawatha" or "Red Cloud" westbound on Colborne St. at Market, late in 1904. Right: the two interurban cars passing at Grand Valley Park about the same time. (OPM)

Right: Combine (later 49 or 50) at the Galt limits connecting with stage for the centre of town, early in 1905. (OPM)

Above: interior of the interurban cars. Left: Looking south along the Grand River from the summit of the hill above Paris, summer of 1904. (OPM)

Above: the Blue Lake trestle. The branch curves away on the skyline left (OPM).
Below: a sylvan section of line just north of Glen Morris, early in 1905.

Looking north down the grade towards Paris, summer of 1904. This view looks the opposite direction from that on page 55. (O PM)

house. No further track was laid, though the company often stated that completion of the branch was about to be undertaken. It was abandoned in 1915 after the Blue Lake power house was closed down in favour of purchased power.

The interurban was generally built on a 24-foot private right-of-way but had heavy grades in places (up to a reported 8%) and pursued a wandering course following the line of least resistance. There were only one or two major freight shippers; coal for the power house was a major freight requirement and was handled entirely over the Blue Lake branch. Efforts were made to interest the Toronto Hamilton & Buffalo to interchange carload freight with the interurban at Brantford but were unavailing.

Late in 1906 a storage battery was installed on a building three miles south of Galt in an effort to maintain voltage at the north end of the line. This was closed down in 1911 when purchased power was adopted at the Galt terminal.

G.V.R. cars originally ran to a waiting room in the Kerby House at Market St. in Brantford, reversing at that point. In May 1910 they were extended to a new crossover at Alfred St. to reduce congestion at Market St. When a waiting room was opened in the former generating station building at Colborne and Clarence Sts. in 1915, interurban cars began running through to Echo Place, and to Mohawk Park in season. In the following year a new waiting station was opened at Colborne & Market Sts. but freight continued to be handled at Clarence St.

FINANCIAL PLIGHT

By 1909 the poor results of the Galt extension were causing problems, even though these were the best years of most interurban lines. The company lost one of its chief assets in January 1911 when its General Manager, W.P. Kellett, became Chief Engineer of the Lake Erie & Northern, and in May 1912 the G.V. Ry. went into receivership. Turmoil then ensued, and the end result was that the City of Brantford assumed ownership as of August 5, 1914.

In the meantime the company was being kept afloat only by neglect of maintenance, as a result of which derailments became common-

GALT

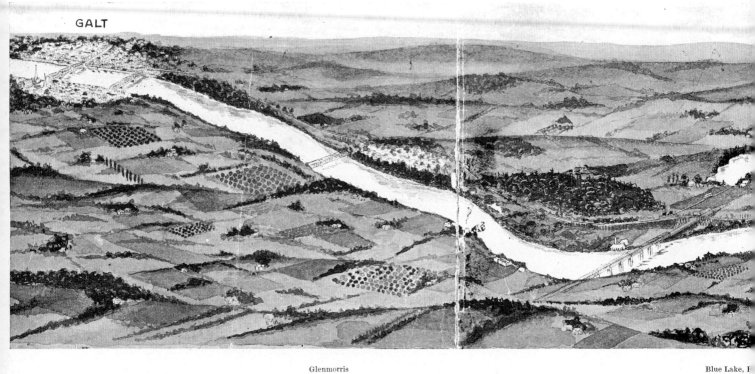

Glenmorris   Blue Lake, I

The consequences of
running too fast
at a sharp curve.
Believed to be near
Blue Lake
about 1912. (OPM)

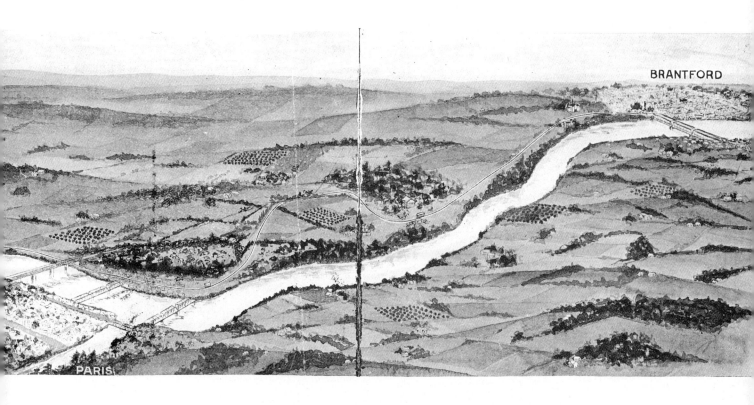

BRANTFORD

PARIS

Car 50 at the Brantford terminus, Kerby House. (OPM)

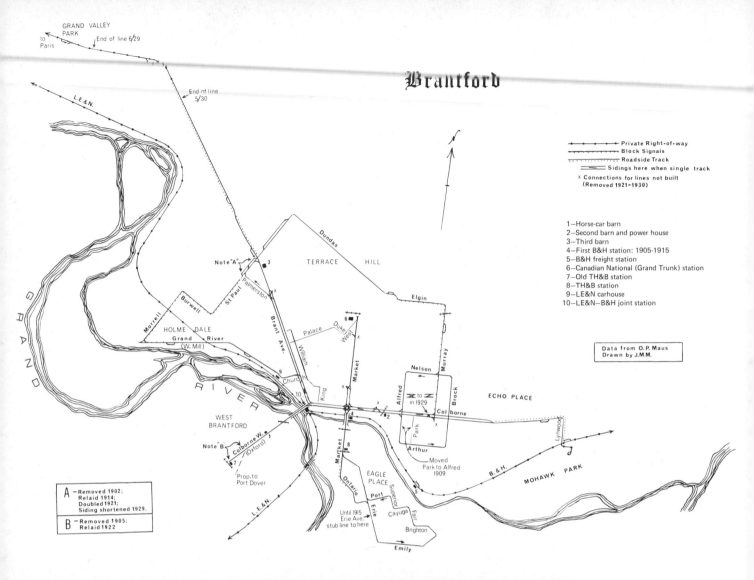

Brantford

Private Right-of-way
Block Signals
Roadside Track
Sidings here when single track
x Connections for lines not built
(Removed 1921-1930)

1—Horse-car barn
2—Second barn and power house
3—Third barn
4—First B&H station: 1905-1915
5—B&H freight station
6—Canadian National (Grand Trunk) station
7—Old TH&B station
8—TH&B station
9—LE&N carhouse
10—LE&N—B&H joint station

Data from O.P. Maus
Drawn by J.M.M.

GRAND VALLEY PARK
to Paris
End of line 6/29
End of line 5/30

L.E.&N.

GRAND RIVER

Note "A"

TERRACE HILL

Dundas

Elgin

St Paul Palmerston

Burwell Morrell

HOLME DALE
Grand River (W. Mill)

Brant Ave.

William

Church

Palace

Duke West

Market

King

Nelson

Murray

Brock

Colborne

ECHO PLACE

to — in 1929

Alfred

Park

Arthur

Moved Park to Alfred 1909

Lynwood

WEST BRANTFORD

Note "B"
Colborne W. (Oxford)

Prop. to Port Dover

Market

Ontario

EAGLE PLACE

Port Superior

Erie

Cayuga

Fall

Brighton

Emily

Until 1915 Erie Ave. stub line to here

B. & H.   MOHAWK PARK

L. E. & N.

A —Removed 1902;
Relaid 1914;
Doubled 1921;
Siding shortened 1929.

B —Removed 1905;
Relaid 1922.

One of the Patterson & Corbin cars, apparently numbered 6, at Mohawk Park. This car does not appear on available equipment lists (OPM).

Right: Two open cars meet at Grand Valley Park in the summer of 1904. (OPM)

Above: Car 82 (ex-36) and express car 210 near Grand Valley Park about 1917. Left: 82 in later years, July 1936. Believed to be the last double-truck open cars in Canada. (OPM)

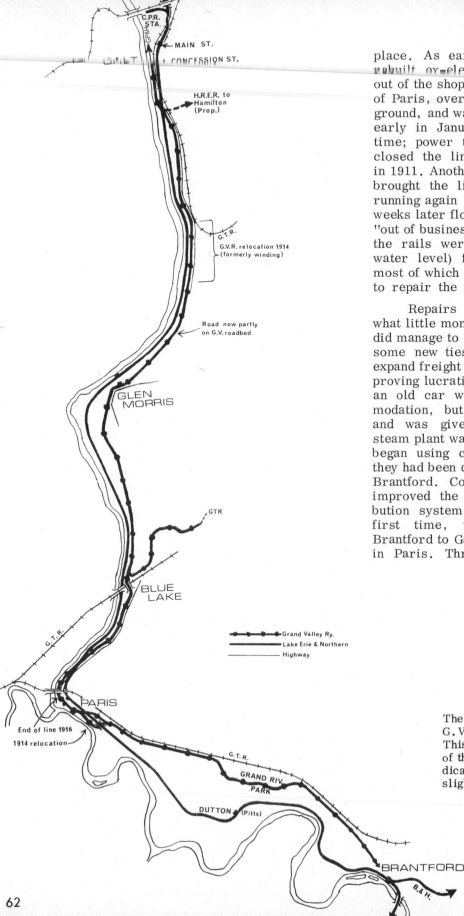

place. As early as January 15, 1908 newly-rebuilt ox-elevated car 56, only three weeks out of the shop, was derailed on a bridge south of Paris, overturned and fell twenty feet to the ground, and was scrapped. A heavy snow storm early in January 1910 closed the line for a time; power troubles at the Blue Lake plant closed the line north of Paris for six weeks in 1911. Another snowstorm in February 1912 brought the line to a standstill. Cars began running again on March 26, but less than two weeks later flooding and washouts put the line "out of business" again at the north end (where the rails were only a few feet above normal water level) from April 8 to July 10, during most of which time the company made no effort to repair the damage.

Repairs and snow-clearing took most of what little money was available, but the Trustee did manage to scrape together enough to install some new ties and ballast, and to attempt to expand freight and express business which was proving lucrative elsewhere. In November 1914 an old car was rebuilt with express accommodation, but the attempt was unsuccessful and was given up in 1918. The Blue Lake steam plant was closed down in 1915 and cars began using commercial power at Paris, as they had been doing for some time at Galt and Brantford. Conversion to commercial power improved the reserve capacity of the distribution system, and on June 6, 1913 for the first time, through cars were scheduled Brantford to Galt, instead of requiring a change in Paris. Through cars were run every two

The L.E.&N. was built close to the older G.V.R. line through the Grand Valley. This map shows the relative locations of the two railways. For the distance indicated, G.V.R. tracks had to be relocated slightly at L.E. & N. expense (JMM).

hours, with hourly service to Paris.

In September 1914 the Blue Lake trestle over the G.T.R. was condemned, even though it was only ten years old. Passengers had to change cars and walk across until it was rebuilt. At this time the height of the bridge was lessened by eight feet to reduce the gradient on the approaches.

GALT LINE ENDS

The City as owner was anxious to be rid of the Galt line, and secured a consulting engineer's report in November 1915 which cited decayed ties, lack of ballast, unsafe trestles and culverts, gaps in fencing, and slack overhead wire. It would cost $43,000 to place it in proper condition and its scrap value was estimated at $20,900. The Paris-Galt section was estimated to have lost $2674 in the first six months of the year, while the line south of Paris had earned $1653. The city therefore accepted an offer from the L.E.&N. to buy it in order to simplify construction and eliminate competition. Traffic on this section was already sparse, and it was found that 45% of through Paris-Galt passengers were travelling on interline tickets to G.P.&H. points, all of which would certainly be diverted to the new line even if the old one kept running. The track north of Paris was therefore sold for $30,000, the city retaining title to the rails and wire on the Blue Lake branch.

The Galt line continued to run until February 3, 1916 when floods piled three feet of ice on the track near Galt and knocked down some poles. This proved to be the end of the Grand Valley Railway, as the Lake Erie & Northern hastily put a single car in service Galt to Brantford in advance of the intended opening date, using the Water St. trackage of the G.V.R. as a temporary entrance to Galt.

A line relocation at the top of the hill above Paris allowed the suburban line to cross under the L.E.&N., and improved both grade and visibility. A new Brantford Municipal station was opened in Paris, and two new cars received from Preston early in 1919. The track was reballasted. Fares were raised in 1916 from 30c to 35c, but were replaced in August 1924 by a zone system with one-man crews.

Abandonment of the Paris line was considered in 1927, but it was determined that less money would be lost if it continued to run than if it did not. However, the end came on June 15, 1929 when buses took over the service, except for a stub at the Brantford end which continued in use for another year.

It is difficult to avoid the conclusion that Ickes in 1903 was looking in the wrong direction. Had he built south into prosperous farming territory instead of north into the Grand River valley, the results might well have been different. As the Lake Erie & Northern was to find out, the territory into which the line was built was the least remunerative in the entire region.

SUMMARY

Figures as reported in Government annual reports for the G.V.R. and the Brantford city line are rather difficult to interpret, owing to the different manner in which they were reported at various times. The B.S.R., G.V.R. and W.T.V.&I. were reported separately until 1908. In 1909 the figures were combined under the G.V.R. name, and starting in 1918 they appear under the Brantford Municipal name. The W.T.V.&I. is not reported separately until 1919; the reason for this is unknown, and is strange because the lines were entirely independent of each other after 1914. Even the Brantford local line figures are not comparable, as those after 1918 include the Paris line, while those pre-1908 do not.

Figures for the Brantford local lines are available from 1901 and show a strangely irregular passenger volume. In the first year 261,000 passengers were reported; by 1906 this had increased to 511,000 but fell off to 402,000 in the next year. The interurban line showed a similar trend, starting with 203,000 passengers in 1904, rising to 257,000 in 1906 and declining to 208,000.

The first year of combined reporting (year ending 30/6/09), 1,026,000 passengers were carried including the W.T.V.&I., which in the last previous year had reported 388,000. This reached a peak of just over 1,600,000 in 1914 and again in 1917. Freight tonnage never exceeded 300 for any year except the first in which any such business was reported (1910) when the figure given was 1464 tons. This seems scarcely credible unless non-revenue coal hauled to the Blue Lake power house had been included in error.

In postwar years, passenger traffic in Brantford increased through the 'twenties. Starting with 1,910,000 in 1918 it increased fairly steadily to a peak of 2,865,000 in 1929; it then fell off to a low of 1,535,000 in 1933 and climbed again to 2,408,000 in 1939. (This omits the year 1932 when passengers carried on the buses during the trial period were not reported by the railway).

The various revenue and expense figures do not entirely bear out the company's tales of extreme financial stringency, though lack of maintenance undoubtedly helped to cut down expenses. The year ending June 30, 1912, during which the interurban line was idle for some months, was one of the more profitable (or perhaps less unprofitable) years in the history of combined G.V.R. accounting; the operating ratio in that year was 79. In 1908, the last year in which the interurban figures can be isolated, the G.V.R. ratio was 92 though in the previous year it had been 78.

After municipal purchase, the Brantford city routes plus the Paris line were profitable until the early 'twenties. Throughout the next decade, the operating ratio (percentage of gross receipts required to pay day-to-day running expenses) was rarely below 91. The onset of the Depression affected the system severely, resulting in a drop of patronage of nearly 20% in one year and increasing the operating ratio from 76 to 91. The city was, however, quite successful in cutting costs to match declining revenues, so that at least the results were no worse in years of lowest traffic than in other years.

Left: "Hiawatha" or "Red Cloud" with rebuilt vestibules, as car 59 of the Toronto & York Radial Railways, January 1921 (HEPC).
Below left: former G.V.R. line on Water St. S. in Galt, 1961 (JDK)
Right: Paris G.V.R. station as it looked in 1961. (JDK)

5

Woodstock, Thames Valley, & Ingersoll

One of the smallest of Canadian inter-urbans, this lived for a quarter of a century in obscurity and has left behind no signs of its existence.

The story of this small line begins in July 1899 with a visit to Woodstock by Mr. S.R. Ickes, of Ickes & Armstrong, Pittsburgh, who was then promoting the Lykens and Williams Valley Street Railway in Pennsylvania. No one knows what attracted him to Woodstock, but he evidently liked what he saw, as he returned and under the corporate name of the Von Echa Co., served as construction contractor on the ten-mile line. (The further fortunes of the Von Echa concern are noted elsewhere in this book.) Ickes & Armstrong put up less than 20% of the capital for the line, the remainder being raised locally.

The track began originally at Wellington St., Woodstock, and ran on Dundas St., Mill

St. and Park Row in order to avoid a level crossing by using an existing underpass under the Grand Trunk main line. Outside Woodstock the tracks were laid on a narrow strip of company-owned land parallel to the south edge of what is now Highway No. 2 through Beach-ville to Ingersoll, operating on Charles West & Oxford Sts. and ending at the Ingersoll Inn.

Tracklaying began on July 3, 1900 and service was started as far as Beachville on November 8 of that year, and in June 1901 was extended to Ingersoll after franchise matters had been settled. A wooden carhouse and a 225 H.P. brick power house faced each other on opposite sides of the track a mile from Woodstock. Station premises were maintained in an office building on the south side of Dundas St. at Broadway. A park was established on the Thames River east of Beachville and christened "Fairmount Park" after the large park of that name in Philadelphia.

Above: Beachville about 1905. The identity of
the car is unknown. (JMM)

There was a fairly steep grade on Dundas
St., with the sharp turn into Mill St. at the
bottom. The difficulty lay in the possibility of
too much speed downhill, and too little uphill
as it was impossible to "get a run at the
grade".

In August 1902 the line was completed to
its full length ($11\frac{1}{2}$ miles) by the opening of the
last short distance between Wellington and
Huron Sts., Woodstock, which had been delayed
pending permission to cross a G.T.R. branch
at grade. The line now ended at the Brewery.

CARS UNKNOWN

Very little information is available on the
cars, but the first report of five (1901) was
increased to seven in subsequent Reports; perhaps by transfer of equipment from Brantford
which came under the same ownership in 1902.
As was the practice on lines controlled by
Ickes, the cars were named rather than numbered, and only three of the seven can be
identified by name. One of them, a small but
ornate vehicle named "Estelle", appears to
have been built as a single-trucker but later
given double trucks. It was undoubtedly second-
hand from some small line in Pennsylvania as
its purchase was arranged through a dealer in
Harrisburg. This was the car that inaugurated
the service, and was named after Dr. Ickes'
daughter. It arrived in Woodstock before it

was needed, and was stored at the G.T.R.
station.

Carload freight service was forbidden by
the charter but would have been unsuccessful
in any case as the area is well served by both
major railways. Newspapers were, however,
carried on the cars and delivered by the
motorman en route.

RECEIVERSHIP

Although sharing common ownership with
the Grand Valley and the Brantford Street Railway, the Woodstock line retained local management. It went into voluntary receivership in
May 1912, and was not included in the 1914
sale of the "parent" G.V.R. It was subsequently
operated by the Manager acting as trustee for
the bondholders, an arrangement that lasted
for the rest of the line's existence.

Fares were raised on May 1920 from 20c
to 25c (single) and bus competition was encountered as soon as the paralleling highways
were paved.

The little railway kept up its hourly
service in complete obscurity. The most serious accident revealed by this researcher was
in 1902 when a heavily-loaded car was derailed
in collision with a pig. Derailments on the
curve at the bottom of the Dundas St. hill also
seem to have been fairly common.

A famous
view of most
of "Estelle".
It is believed that
this view
was taken when
the line opened,
evidently
a solemn occasion.
(RJS)

A 6% semi-annual dividend in the early days was converted into a deficit for the 1922-23 fiscal year of $1135, a large sum for a company whose gross revenue was in the order of $25,000 per annum.

Abandonment came on August 16, 1925 when company-owned buses took over. The railway company continued to operate the buses until 1942 when it sold its operating rights and went out of business.

Since figures were not separately reported from 1909 to 1918, complete data is not available. Passenger loads in the first year were reported at 110,000, rising to 397,000 in 1907. After separate reporting was resumed, loads had slipped badly to 83,000 in 1920 and 69,000 in the last full year, 1924. Despite this, a deficit on operations (before fixed charges) was never encountered. Milk, express and newspaper revenue did not exceed $1600 per year.

Below: "Estelle" in Woodstock at an unknown date. (RJS)

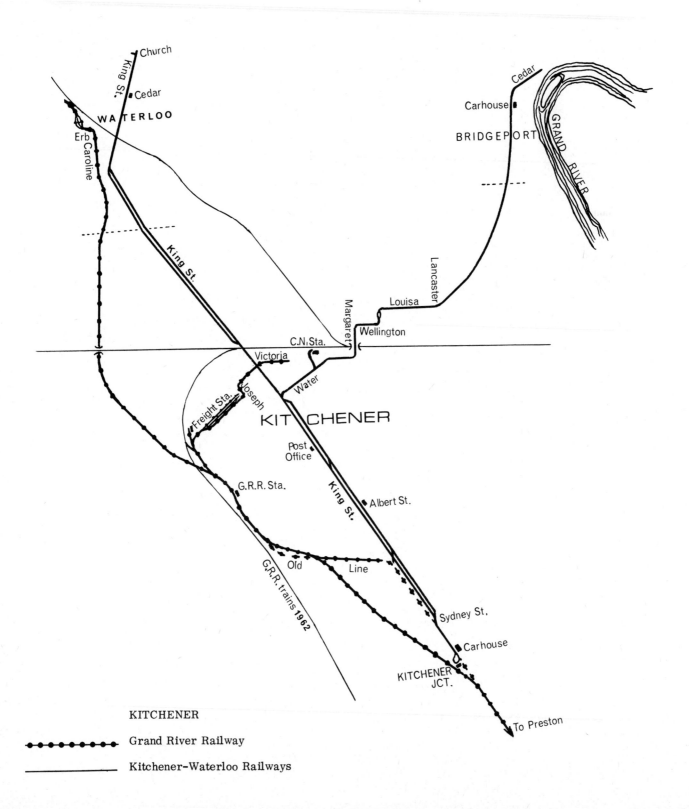

Church

Cedar

King St.

WATERLOO

Erb

Caroline

King St.

Cedar

Carhouse

BRIDGEPORT

GRAND RIVER

Lancaster

Louisa

Wellington

Margaret

C.N. Sta.

Victoria

Water

Freight Sta.

Joseph

KITCHENER

Post
Office

G.R.R. Sta.

Albert St.

King St.

G.R.R. trains 1962

Old

Line

Sydney St.

Carhouse

KITCHENER
JCT.

To Preston

KITCHENER

●━●━●━● Grand River Railway

──────── Kitchener-Waterloo Railways

6

Berlin & Waterloo Street Railway, Kitchener - Waterloo Railways

The first public transportation in the towns of Waterloo and Berlin (now Kitchener) was provided by the Berlin & Waterloo Street Railway which was incorporated in 1886. The President, Treasurer and Manager were collectively one man, Col. Thomas M. Burt. $2\frac{1}{2}$ miles of line was opened in 1888, extending from Berlin Town Hall at Scott St. along King St. to Cedar St. in Waterloo. A short spur ran to the Grand Trunk station on Water St., and the street cars carried the mail for many years to the Post Office on King St. near the town hall.

27-lb. flat rail was used in paved sections, though 30-lb. T-rail was used in dirt sections, and the track was laid close to the north edge of the pavement. A year after opening, the little company owned eight cars, both open and closed, and 17 horses, also three large covered sleighs for winter use. Half-hourly service was given. The stables and car shed were at the Cedar St. end of the line.

Each horse carried a small bell whose tinkling warned prospective passengers of the car's approach. The last trip of the day was signalled by a larger bell with a deeper tone.

ELECTRIFICATION

In March 1893 the company secured permission to electrify. Owing to the small amount of capital available, this process took over two years and the first electric car did not run until May 18, 1895. Power was purchased from the Berlin Gas Co. which installed a new Edison generator for railway purposes. The existing track was bonded and reballasted.

The first cars used were three of the former closed horse cars, modified for electric traction. New vestibules were added and Peckham electric trucks provided. Two of the cars had a single Westinghouse 25 H.P. motor,

Electric car 2 on the main line passes a horse car bound for the G.T.R. station not yet electrified. (KWR)

while the third had two GE No. 800 motors and was used in peak periods hauling the horse cars behind it.

The old horse-car rails proved unsuitable for the greater stresses of electric operation, and the condition of the trackage rapidly became critical. The management had not expected to have to replace the light rail for about three years, and was unwilling to meet the cost of immediate rebuilding. Therefore the company was sold in 1896 to a new group headed by a member of the prominent Breithaupt family. The new management bought four new cars (two open cars by Ottawa and two closed cars by Canadian General Electric of Peterborough) but only two Peckham trucks were provided; after the custom of the time the trucks were switched from closed to open bodies and back again twice a year.

The light rail was replaced by 56-lb. T-rails and it was probably at this time that the single track was centred on the street. There was a passing track in Berlin between Ontario and Young Streets.

NEW CARS

About 1899 four ex-horse cars, two closed and two open, were bought from an unknown source. The two closed cars, which differed in appearance, became motor cars 5 and 6, while the open cars became trailers 7 and 8, It is also quite possible that 7 and 8 were actually ex-Berlin horse cars only now given numbers in the electric series.

Another change in management in 1901 resulted in the purchase of more cars; one new one built by Ottawa (No. 9), the first double-trucker in the city, and two more second-hand (from Buffalo) which became closed car 12 and open car 14. Car 11 was built for the Bridgeport line, and the number 10 was left open, for reasons unknown, until 1908. Apparently a revised numbering system had been adopted by the new 1901 management, beginning with the 1896-built cars which are known to have later been 1, 2, 3 and 4: presumably the converted horse cars had by then been disposed of.

Above: Car 2 on King Street at Erb,
Berlin. (KWR) This scene has not
changed much in 75 years (left, WH)
Below: at the Grand Trunk station.
Note omnibus backed up to the platform
in background.

Left: car 20 in later years after rebuilding for Pay-As-You-Enter service, a process that obviously weakened the Platforms. Below: Car 18 in original condition as Saint John Railway 51. (RRB)

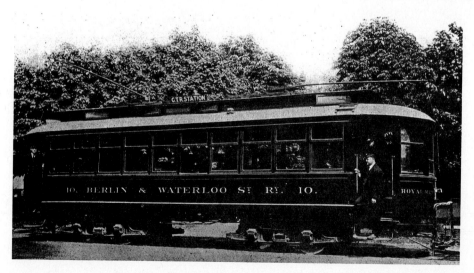

Car 10 when new. As suggested by "Royal Mail" on the dash, its normal assignment was to the G.T.R. station run, where it carried mail sacks to the downtown Post Office. (JMM)

Left: Converted horse car 5 preceded by a similar car with two trailers, 1895 (RRB)
Right: The original car barn just after electrification, 1895 (RRB)

In 1902 a short extension from Scott St. to Albert St. (now Madison Ave.) in Berlin reached a new car house. This replaced the original car shed in Waterloo, which had been expanded as recently as 1898.

A note has been found that ex-Toronto horse cars 30 and 188 came to Berlin in 1904. This is not confirmed by Toronto records, which state that these cars, converted to electricity, were transferred to the Mimico line in that year. However, after appearing on the Toronto & York Radial (Mimico) records for the year 1904 only, no further record is found, so that it is conceivable that they might have been passed on to Berlin. It is certain that trailer 58 did come from Toronto in 1904, and remained in existence, latterly as a sort of historical relic, until 1944. It was never renumbered and it is therefore possible that 30 and 188 might also have run in Berlin for a few years without being given a distinctive Berlin number.

MUNICIPAL OWNERSHIP

Early in 1905 a steam power house was opened adjacent to the new carhouse, and the company stopped buying power from the Gas Company, which had been city-owned since June 1903. It was perhaps this successful venture into municipal ownership that caused the town of Berlin to consider taking over the street railway. However, there was no precedent for one municipality (Berlin) expropriating property that lay in another (Waterloo). Eventually a settlement between the two towns was reached, the purchase was approved by Berlin

voters and on May 1, 1907 the town became owner of the railway at a cost of about $80,000.

At first, management of the line was exercised by the Light Commissioners but in 1909 was taken over directly by the Town Council. Eventually it was placed under the Public Utilities Commission.

The town undertook a number of improvements, constructing the first double track (Water St. to Albert St. in Berlin) and replacing the steam power house by purchased Hydro power from Niagara Falls. Additional cars were purchased: one new one (No. 10) from Ottawa and three well-travelled but little-used cars from Saint John, N.B. (16-18-20). These had been built by the Montreal Park & Island Railway in 1900 but sold to Saint John in 1903. They turned out to be too large for use there and came as virtually new cars to Berlin in 1908.

PAY AS YOU ENTER

A short time later they were modified for Pay-as-you-Enter service. This was a "radical" new idea in which the conductor, instead of following a passenger to his seat to collect the fare, was stationed on the rear platform and collected it as passengers boarded. In 1912 two Preston "Prairie Type" cars (familiar throughout Western Canada as the nickname suggests) were bought already equipped for P.A.Y.E. fare collection. A 10-minute service was begun and the new fare system inaugurated with these five cars on April 1, 1913.

In order to make the increased frequency possible, double track replaced single track from the G.T.R. crossing in Berlin to Union St., and car storage capacity at the Albert St. barn was increased. The line now had 5.1 miles of track; it owned 19 cars of which six were not in use.

In 1919 the first single-end cars arrived (the "Prairie Types" were later converted). These were three second-hand P.A.Y.E. cars

from Cleveland. The single track in Waterloo was extended a short distance to Church St. where a wye was built which remained in use for the life of the line. At the other end, however, great changes were being made. Since 1903 the interurban cars of the Preston & Berlin line, and its successor the Grand River Railway, had been running from Albert St., downtown over K/W rails. Between Sterling Ave. and the City Limit, the single interurban track was laid on the south side of the street.

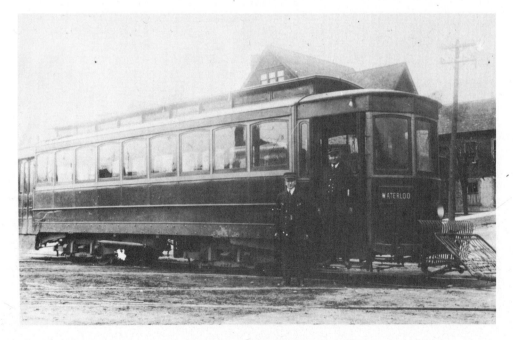

Above left: Car 16 on King St. (KWR)
Above right: King St., 1920 (JMM).

One of the three single-end cars (26, 28, 30) bought from Cleveland in 1919 (KWR)

After the franchise expired on October 8, 1919, the K/W extended its service over the G.R.R. single track to a wye at Maple Lane, 400 feet short of the City Limit. There was a period of 18 months when both companies were apparently running over this section, until the G.R.R. opened its new line which by-passed the street section. This was opened in May 1921, following which the street railway double-tracked the section between Albert and Sydney Streets, leaving only two blocks of the old roadside line at the outer end. A station, called Kitchener Junction, was opened at the end of the line in October 1921, becoming the major transfer point between interurban and city cars. The wye was before long replaced by a loop.

At this point the Berlin & Bridgeport line was taken over, so its history must now be recounted.

Above: 24 running east on King St., Kitchener, in 1943 (KWR)

"Prairie Type" 24. Note that these cars were not rebuilt for 1-man operation, as was almost invariably done elsewhere. (JDK)

Car 62, one of two
built in 1922
for the Bridgeport
line, in downtown
Kitchener, 1943.
(KWR)

BERLIN & BRIDGEPORT

The Berlin & Bridgeport Electric Street Railway was promoted by the Berlin & Waterloo line, and it was built by B. & W. forces, as the first stage of a line to Elora and Fergus. It was incorporated in 1901 and opened 1.45 miles of track on July 14, 1902 from a junction with the B. & W. on Water St. to a sugar refinery on the northeast outskirts of the town; shortly afterwards, the rest of the line was opened as far as Bridge and Cedar Sts., Bridgeport, a total of 2.7 miles. Bridgeport cars used B. & W. rails to reach the Berlin town hall, in later years reversing near Scott St.

One car was purchased in 1902, a double-truck car numbered 11 in the B. & W. series, built by A.C. Larivière, a small firm whose products were almost unknown outside of Montreal. How this one car came so far afield is unknown.

There was only one passing track on the line, between Louisa and Wellington Sts. in Berlin. The line crossed the G.T.R. main line on an overhead bridge on Margaret Ave., and there was nearly a mile of private right-of-way beyond Lancaster St., Berlin.

The line was run by a large storage battery in off hours, at which times service was given by a small car rented from the

B. & W. When the town took over the latter in 1907, the Bridgeport company was not included and assumed independent operation, though power continued to be purchased.

FINANCIAL PROBLEMS

In 1912 the company changed its name to "Berlin & Northern Railway" and in 1919 to "Waterloo-Wellington Railway" and hopes of constructing the line on to Fergus were kept alive, in legal terms at least. All was not well, however; post-war inflation had hit the little company hard. The management wished to dispose of the railway before the end of the franchise period (1922) but the only probable purchaser, the city of Kitchener, was unwilling to take over an obvious "white elephant". The Bridgeport fare was almost doubled early in December 1920, going from 5c to 12 tickets for $1.00, which caused intense indignation in the area. The Ontario Railway & Municipal Board was brought into the picture, and ordered the fare reduced except that a double fare could be charged in winter months to inter-town passengers. The fare zone was at Lancaster St.

The company had to accept this order, but it was very unhappy and on February 1, 1921 reduced service to two trips a day for a short time.

In the midst of all this (no doubt in the forlorn hope of increasing the value of the property), the management announced that

Above: Car 40 meets a Grand River Railway
train at Kitchener Jct., August 1946 (JDK).
Right: Car 12 converted for one-man. (JMM)

plans were being developed for an extension to Guelph. This was said to propose making use of five miles of line eastwards from Bridgeport which had been graded in 1910 by the People's Railway, an ambitious interurban scheme that completed nothing and evaporated in a cloud of financial mismanagement about 1912.

Finally the end of the franchise period approached, and Kitchener prepared to take over the line. The purchase was defeated by the voters in May 1922, but the question being put again, was approved on August 18 and the line passed under the control of the Kitchener-Waterloo Railway though legal formalities were not completed for another two years. The city immediately cancelled the two-zone fare but maintained an extra charge for transfers to the main line in Kitchener. A small carhouse was built in Bridgeport and two modified single-truck Birney cars bought.

PETER WITTS ARRIVE

The immediate post-war years were noteworthy not only for the changes at the Kitchener end of the main line (already mentioned) and for the acquisition of the Bridgeport line but for other reasons as well: construction of a modern carhouse, surprisingly large for a railway of this size, adjacent to the Kitchener Jct. terminal, and the purchase of five large two-man Peter Witt cars. These had been built by Cleveland Railways to handle wartime traffic, but arrived after the end of the war. They were not well liked in Cleveland, and were sold between 1922 and 1924. Possibly the

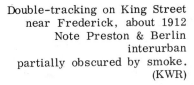

Double-tracking on King Street
near Frederick, about 1912
Note Preston & Berlin
interurban
partially obscured by smoke.
(KWR)

Above: The new carhouse under construction, July 1923. Below: Car 38 in downtown Kitchener about 1943. (KWR)

Peter Witt car 32 (ex-Cleveland 1096) at Kitchener Junction (JDK)

uneven flooring, which ramped up over each truck and down again at the doors, was partly responsible. At any rate, these cars remained base-service equipment in Kitchener and were never converted for one-man service as was almost invariably the case in other cities of Kitchener's size. Identical cars ran in London, Ont., later going to Saskatoon.

The arrival of the Witts permitted many of the older cars to be scrapped or converted for other uses, and made possible the establishment of a five-minute headway. In order to make this possible, double track was extended from Union St. to William St., Waterloo, leaving only three short stretches of single track on the main line, and these were never doubled.

In 1928 the last addition to the roster was made when a Birney car was purchased second-hand from Peterborough, Ont. Since one indication on the old route linen ("C.N.R. Depot") was useable in Kitchener, the sign was frugally left in place and the car always used on that line, carrying the mail to the Post Office as had been the case since horse-car days. When the station spur was abandoned, car 66 was retired.

BUS SERVICE

In May 1939 the first bus operation was started by buying out a small private crosstown operation. Finding the buses to their liking, the city abandoned the Bridgeport line in the same year. In 1940 a new post office was opened, and since this was not on the street railway, trucks began carrying the mail, and

Sweeper 16 at work on the Bridgeport line. Note the surprisingly rural territory along this line. (KWR)

the C.N.R. Depot line was abandoned in 1941. These reduced track mileage from 10.35 to 6.00 which remained constant until the end.

The street cars would all have been replaced at about this time if it had not been for the war; as it turned out they continued to run for five years longer. During this time maintenance was cut to the absolute minimum until the entire street railway presented a sorry sight (and sound) indeed. The conversion date was fixed for December 31, 1946, the first post-war conversion in Canada and the first installation of the "new breed" of trolley coaches manufactured by Canadian Car & Foundry Co. at Fort William.

SUDDEN END

However, nature took a hand, in the form of a severe sleet storm on the evening of December 27 which cut the power and brought down the worn-out trolley wire at three points. With no cars running, the tracks rapidly became impassable owing to packed ice and snow. It was not deemed worth while to put the cars back in service for just four days, so they were pushed one by one into the Kitchener Jct. loop and roadside track where they would not disrupt traffic, and left to themselves.

The new trolley-coach overhead was erected above the street-car wire; the service interruption gave the line crews time to remove the old wire with ease, and the new vehicles began running as scheduled on New Year's Day. The entire fleet of street cars was sold for scrap in March, 1947. As a post-script, it might be observed that the trolley-coach system itself was scrapped in 1973.

SUMMARY

This was one of the most profitable street railways in Canada. Figures are available from 1896 to 1946, an unusually long span, and show that the least profitable years were those usually expected to be the most lucrative: the earliest, and those of World War II. During half a century, in only one year (ending June 30, 1904) did an operating deficit occur. Between 1907 and 1943 the operating ratio (percentage of receipts required to pay day-to-day operating costs) exceed 80 only twice; however previous to 1907 it dropped below 80 only once. The explanation may be, in part at least, that figures for the Bridgeport line were included up to 1906, but separated from 1907 to 1926.

(Contrary to what might be expected from the statements of its management, however, the Bridgeport line never had an operating deficit in all its years of separate reporting. In fact, its operating ratio tended to fall in later years and was at its lowest in the last year when it stood at 57.)

In only one year (1910) did the Berlin & Waterloo line report any freight at all; in that year it reported 280 tons from which a gross revenue of $14 was said to be derived. "Mail and Express", however, figured in earnings from 1898 to 1946 and while the gross was usually under $2000, it reached a peak of $5300 in 1929 and stayed above $4500 until 1939 when it fell off with the end of mail service. It is the passenger figures that hold our interest. Omitting minor fluctuations, these reveal a steady buildup that was interrupted only briefly by the Depression. It is best demonstrated by a short tabulation:

Year	Passengers
1896:	205,000
1904:	548,000
1914:	1,168,000
1919:	1,532,000
1924:	2,660,000
1929:	3,291,000
1935:	2,121,000
1940:	4,190,000 (includes buses)

In 1942 separate figures show 3,561,000 passengers on the one car line and 3,780,000 on the buses. In the final year of rail operation, this had risen to 4,720,000 by street car and 9,292,000 by bus; the enormous increase in total passengers caused by the expansion of the "K/W" area will be noted.

Above: Car 2 rests at the end of the
line (KWR)
Centre: Car 38 on King Street at
Frederick about 1925. Note uneven
floor line characteristic of these cars
(KWR)
Right: Interior of car 10 (KWR)
Opposite: The end of the line, Kitchener
Junction, January 1947 (JDK)

Above: St. George's
Square on an
unknown occasion
about 1898.
Left: On the Square
in early days. (OPM)
The badly-faded
original of this
photo was found many
years later
in the rafters of the
Brantford carhouse.

7

Guelph Radial Railway

The origins of this line go back to August 1894, when a 30-year franchise for a street railway in Guelph was granted to George Sleeman, proprietor of the Silver Creek Brewery. The brewery had been established in 1851 by his father, and the family lived in a large house known as "The Manor" nearby. The Sleemans built well; in 1971 the Brewery, the Manor and the 1895 carhouse were all still standing. Mr. Sleeman died in 1926, having served as Mayor on three separate occasions.

In 1895 the Guelph Railway Co. was formed with George Sleeman as President and E. Sleeman as Secretary-Treasurer and Superintendent. Five miles of track were built, using 56-lb. rails purchased in Chicago. The first spike was driven on May 17, 1895 and 20-minute service began on September 17 of

the same year. (The official opening was the following day.) All cars started from the railway stations at the foot of Carden St. and ran to three widely-separated parts of the town: to the Ontario Agricultural College at the end of Dundas St. (this line was built beside the road); to the Brewery on Waterloo Ave., and to Woodlawn Cemetary on Elora Rd.

A power house was built on Sleeman-owned land on Surrey St. downtown and a stone carhouse on Waterloo Ave. near the brewery. Two open and three closed cars were built in Peterborough by Canadian General Electric, and a trailer was obtained from an unknown source.

A small park was opened in 1904 near the end of Waterloo Ave. and called "Riverside Park". A dam built by the brewery had

The GUELPH Radial Ry. Co. J. J. Hackney Mgr. ONE FARE TO OR FROM RINK

STREET RAILWAY RINK Lady's Ticket

ONE FARE TO OR FROM RINK The GUELPH Radial Ry. Co. J. J. Hackney Mgr.

Many Guelph photographs
were taken
at St. George's Square.
This one is from
about 1910. (BMcC)

created a pond nearby, and swimming and skating were featured according to the season. A small admission fee was charged, and coupon tickets were sold for two-way transportation plus admission to the park. The company also operated toboggan slides on the heights behind the carhouse, to which admission was also charged.

It is said that a barrel of beer with handy dipper was maintained at the brewery for convenience of the street railway men, and that some notably speedy trips on the Waterloo Ave. line resulted. Interestingly, some of the sidewalk near the Manor was paved with beer bottles of various colours, embedded neck downwards in concrete, and remained thus for over half a century until the road was widened.

EXPANSION

In 1896, another line was built, from Wyndham St. via Suffolk, Arnold and Paisley Sts. and Edinburgh Rd. to Waterloo Ave. This involved an awkward level crossing over the Grand Trunk main line, and before long (on a date unfortunately unknown), operations were terminated north of the railway, and the tracks to the south were abandoned.

In 1899 the company designed an improved fender which was used not only in Guelph but in Sarnia and Montreal and elsewhere, and was recommended for use in Toronto. A working model of the Sleeman fender is preserved

in the museum at Elora, Ontario.

In the following year the company began carload freight business, and built a small four-wheel locomotive using G.E. 1200 motors, the most powerful then available. An interchange with the G.T.R. was installed, and a large loop built at the Agricultural College in 1902 partly to allow the railway to switch carloads of coal into the College (up to 250 loads a year at peak). Until a larger engine was obtained, there was always some doubt as to whether the coal car would be successfully propelled up the hill near the College.

The railway's busiest period occurred in June each year when gala celebrations encouraged farmers to visit O.A.C. and learn of improved farming methods. As many as 3500 passengers would be carried from the railway stations to the College at this time, and for this traffic the open cars built in 1895 were retained as trailers for many years.

MUNICIPAL OWNERSHIP

In 1902 the company sold out to new owners, who changed its name to Guelph Radial Railway with power to build extensions to Berlin, Mount Forest, Erin, Preston and Puslinch Lake. A line to Puslinch Lake and Preston was planned for some years, but just how much of the rest represented a genuine intention to build, and how much was a desire to increase the value of the company for resale is not known. Only a year after purchasing the line, the owners sold out to the town and the railway was thereafter municipally owned. The town paid $30,000 for the stock and assumed liability for the outstanding debt of $48,000.

Passenger loads doubled between 1902 and 1906, and therefore an extension was added to the carhouse and two single-truck open cars purchased from Montreal. These were Montreal Street Railway 127 and 133, and were joined by a third (163) in 1908. All of these cars had been built in 1893 by the St. Charles Omnibus Co. of Belleville, Ont. They must have been found inadequate or unsuccessful in Guelph as they seem to have been disposed of within ten years.

Expansion continued as in February 1911 the company's power house was closed down and power was purchased from the Niagara distribution system of Ontario Hydro. At the same time a 27-ton freight locomotive was built by Preston Car & Coach Co. from parts supplied by Baldwin Locomotive Works. The first two double-truck passenger cars also arrived: Preston "Prairie Type" cars which were surprisingly large for a small street railway. They had the triple-arch window in the centre of the body which was virtually a trademark of the "Prairie Type". The order was repeated in 1913 (one car) and 1914 (two cars); the total of five was enough to provide normal service on all lines. Some older cars were therefore disposed of; it is apparent from statistical returns that the company owned more cars than are accounted for by the original purchase plus the ex-Montreal cars but information is totally lacking.

MORE FREIGHT HANDLED

In December 1911 a new line was opened for freight service via Surrey and Ontario Sts. to the water works on York Rd.; in the following year this was extended another 3/4-mile out York Rd. and passenger service begun. In 1915 tracks on Suffolk St. were extended west to form an interchange with the Guelph Junction Ry., which was city-owned but operated by the Canadian Pacific. Thereafter, whenever possible Radial freight was interchanged with C.P. because part of the revenue eventually returned to the City through its ownership of the Guelph Junction. Physical limitations prevented this, however, in the case of O.A.C., the largest single shipper.

This was caused by the inability of railway cars to negotiate sharp street-corner curves, plus differences in wheel and flange characteristics. Unless specially built for the purpose, street railways could usually handle interchange freight only where a long straight stretch of track happened to coincide with the existence of potential shippers.

In 1917 the Toronto Suburban interurban line from Toronto was at last opened. T.S.R. cars used Radial rails to reach their terminal at the Grand Trunk station, where a siding was built by the Radial as a layover point for Toronto cars. Despite the voltage difference, Guelph cars used T.S.R. tracks to reach Speedwell Hospital, a temporary wartime institution on the grounds of Guelph Reformatory.

Lower Wyndham St., from a post card mailed in 1913. (BMcC)

Left: "Prairie Type"
car 100,
December 1920. (HEPC)
Below: The Square again,
about 1914. (RJS)

St. George's Square, Post Office and
Upper Wyndham Street. Guelph, Ont., Canada

This service ended when the Hospital was closed, November 8, 1920.

By this time most of the system was laid with 60-lb. rail in gravel ballast, though some 44-lb. rail remained on the O.A.C. loop (the two sides not used for freight) and the outer end of Elora Rd. which was laid beside the road. The outer ends of Waterloo Ave. and York Rd. had virtually open-track construction on unpaved streets. There was a certain amount of 80-lb. rail on concrete slab, but the design had not envisaged the 25-ton weight of the "Prairie Type" cars and the foundation was showing numerous failures particularly under rail joints, causing rough track and poor electrical continuity. The layout was such that service could not be provided more frequently than every 25 minutes.

HERE I AM -- WHO WANTS ME?

Following the War there was a resurgence of interest in interurban railway construction and the Guelph system was coveted by two much larger concerns: the Grand River Railway which was planning to extend north-east from Hespeler on behalf of the C.P.R., and

Ontario Hydro which was hoping to build a Hamilton-Guelph-Elmira Hydro-Radial line. These two interests came into head-on collision at a municipal election on August 11, 1919 when a lease proposal by the Grand River was voted upon. The H.E.P.C. Chairman and chief planner of the Hydro-Radial scheme, Sir Adam Beck, campaigned actively against the proposal which was defeated at the polls. There was also the fear that C.P.R. control through its subsidiary might divert freight from the Radial switching operation.

A careful inventory of the property was made at this time, which gives an interesting picture of what it took to run a small street railway in 1920. Besides the Superintendent ($200 per month), the Master Mechanic ($140) and the Roadmaster ($120), the company employed 10 motormen, 12 conductors, 19 track men, 8 barn men, 3 cleaners and 3 office staff. In the repair shop were a 10-foot lathe, a 12" drill press, a "power hack saw", a 4'x5' iron table saw, emery wheel, acetylene welding outfit, forge and anvil, sand dryer, babbitting mandrel, electric hand drill, 2-ton pit jack, 12-foot 2-ton crane with chain block, and five assorted jacks. All power tools except the hand drill were powered by a 10-H.P. 500-volt motor through shafting and leather belts.

HYDRO TAKES OVER

On July 1, 1920, management of the Guelph Radial was assumed by the Railways Dept. of Ontario Hydro, acting as operating agent for the City. This step had been approved by the voters on the understanding that the Radial would become part of a long Hydro-Radial line. However the Hydro-Radial scheme was rejected in other municipalities, and the proposed line was never built.

Nevertheless, the property was "bought" by Hydro. The standard financial arrangements for Hydro operation had assumed either new construction or purchase from private owners, on behalf of the municipalities. Therefore, all capital expenditures, including purchase, were financed by Hydro bonds, but were backed by deposit of the same amount in municipal bonds, bearing the same interest, which the Commission collected. What was certainly not contemplated was that the Hydro commission would purchase a line from a municipality in order to operate it on behalf of that municipality.

Light freight motor 26, Dec. 1920 (HEPC)

This was not precisely the original intention in Guelph, of course, but after the failure of the Hydro-Radial proposal that is in fact what happened; in the words of a subsequent report on the matter, "the city . . . was required to issue its own debentures for that amount in order to guarantee the Commission that it (the Commission) would have funds out of which to pay the city". This situation must have been virtually unique in street railway history, and was complicated by the fact that the Commission proceeded to spend large sums in rehabilitation for which the city was legally responsible, but for which municipal bonds were not deposited with Hydro.

IMPROVEMENTS

The Hydro management introduced the first Sunday service on July 25, 1921 and raised fares from 5c to 6c on November 1, 1922. The Guelph Radial name was dropped and the rather anonymous "Hydro-Electric Railways" lettered on the cars, which was a severe blow to local pride. Realizing that the Preston cars were too large for conditions in Guelph, Hydro provided seven of their special double-door Birneys (others served in Windsor) and sent the "Prairie Types" to the Scarborough suburban line in Toronto, then also under Hydro management.

New track on concrete foundations, using 85-lb. or 100-lb. rail, was laid on much of the system; some of the 85-lb. material was surplus from the Queenston construction railway. The introduction of such heavily-built track at the same time as lighter four-wheel cars were built was later condemned as extravagance when the time came for the city to pay for it, but seems to be accounted for by the

Two views of Car 221, July 1935 above, and October 1937 below (OPM). The body of Birney car 225 has been acquired by the Rockwood railway museum. It has been roughly treated during its years as a private house and the planned restoration will be a very long and costly project.

fact that Hydro simply used the same form of track construction they were then using on a large scale in Windsor.

New sidings were built on Ontario St., Gordon St. and Elora Rd. to allow more frequent service to be operated, and trackage was altered so that instead of running around St. George's Square, the cars ran through the centre to form a convenient traffic-free transfer point. A new C.P.R. Station was opened in 1925 and street car service to the old one was discontinued.

NOW I HAVE YOU, I DON'T WANT YOU

After plans for the Hydro-Radial scheme were given up, the Commission was not anxious to remain in the local transportation business. Therefore on January 4, 1926 the voters approved taking the system back from Hydro, but on March 8 defeated the necessary bond issue to repay the cost of improvements made to the railway. Since the taxpayers were liable for the deficits whoever operated it, the only direct result of taking it back would be the addition of carrying charges on the "improvement" bonds, so there was little incentive for the voters to approve; this particular point delayed a solution of the matter for another 13 years.

The first bus service was established on September 13, 1926 in a section of the city not served by the railway; the one bus was obtained on loan from Windsor. The experiment was considered successful, and a new Gotfredson bus was bought for Guelph while the ex-Windsor vehicle went on to still another Hydro-managed

line in Peterborough.

In 1930 Puslinch Lake, owned for years by the railway in hopes of building an extension there, was sold and in the following year the first operating loss since the introduction of one-man cars appeared. Three more buses were bought and on August 13, 1930 the Suffolk St. line was replaced owing to the condition of the tracks. One of the seven Birneys was thus rendered surplus and was sent to Windsor. About this time part of the O.A.C. loop was removed and all cars ran up College Ave. to a stop near the MacDonald Institute.

In 1933 the voters again approved the principle of taking the railway back, but again refused to sanction the necessary bond issue. The operating deficit was now a major expense for the city, and railway affairs took up a large proportion of Council debating time. On April 30, 1934 the Hydro Railways Dept. was abolished and the line came under the general supervision of the Hamilton Street Railway, which had become the only other Hydro-controlled railway.

By 1936 the annual deficit, including fixed charges, had reached almost $40,000 (the total deficit since 1920 was now $430,300). In an effort to reduce this, it was decided to end the passenger service on September 30, 1937 and all the remaining lines were discontinued at once. Carload freight to O.A.C. and several downtown industries was continued.

On July 1, 1939 the City at last took the transportation system over, paying the Hydro Commission $321,750, and formed the Guelph Transportation Commission to operate it. Rail

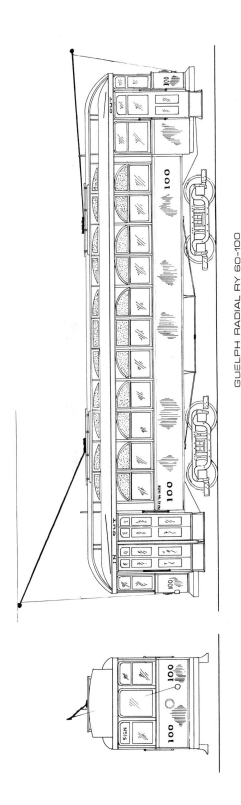

GUELPH RADIAL RY 60-100

Car 70 running as No. 151 on the Scarborough suburban line in Toronto, 1928. (NB)

freight service was discontinued as soon as alternative arrangements could be made.

SUMMARY

Unlike its near neighbour Kitchener, the street railway in Guelph was financially unsuccessful except in the early years. It was reasonably profitable only from 1906 to about 1915, and ran at a deficit every year from 1931 onwards. Passenger loads amounted to 300,000 for the first year for which figures are available (year ending June 30, 1901) and increased to 632,000 in five years. They remained relatively steady until 1911 when another increase took the figure to about 1,200,000 where it remained until Depression years with the exception of a short "peak" period which reached almost 1½ million in 1927. Depression conditions caused a decline to a low of 845,000 in 1933, after which a slow increase had reached 936,000 when rail service ended.

Freight revenues were reported annually, but in many of the years the actual tonnage handled was omitted from the reports. Revenues did not exceed $2000 until 1914 (representing a tonnage of not over 12,500); then about $4250 was earned until the mid 'twenties when a great increase occurred, to a considerable extent owing to a building programme at O.A.C. A peak of $10,000 (probably about 50,000 tons) was reached in 1930-32. The Depression did not affect this aspect of the operation, and it returned over $9000 in 1938 but was discontinued because of a desire to eliminate the roadside tracks on Dundas St. and to rebuild the Speed River bridge without tracks.

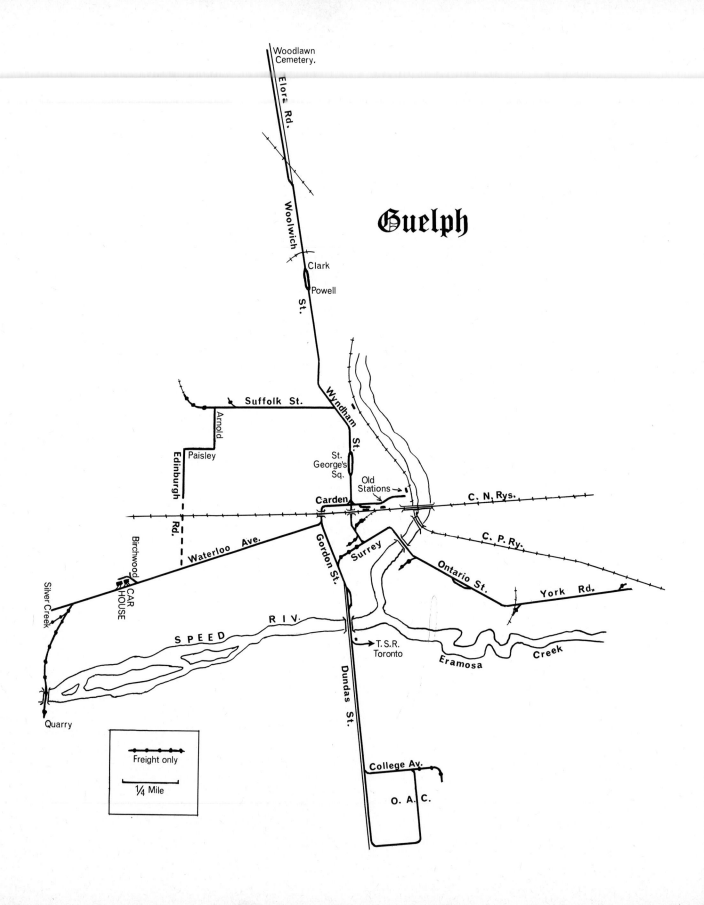

Woodlawn
Cemetery.

Elora Rd.

Woolwich St.

Clark
Powell

Guelph

Wyndham St.

Suffolk St.

Arnold
Paisley

Edinburgh Rd.

St.
George's
Sq.

Old
Stations

Carden

C. N. Rys.

C. P. Ry.

Waterloo Ave.

Gordon St.

Surrey

Ontario St.

York Rd.

Birchwood

CAR
HOUSE

Silver Creek

SPEED RIV.

Dundas St.

T. S. R.
Toronto

Eramosa Creek

Quarry

Freight only

¼ Mile

College Av.

O. A. C.

8

Preston Car & Coach Company

The Preston Car & Coach Co. was a local promotion that enjoyed a comparatively short but busy life from 1908 to 1923. These years happened to coincide with the period of greatest prosperity and expansion for electric lines, so that Preston products were bought in quantity and were found from coast to coast in Canada.

Unlike some firms, the company was prepared to undertake the smallest orders, sometimes for only a single car. It therefore often built for the smaller street railways for whom cheapness was a consideration. When the purchaser was prepared to pay the price of quality, however, Preston products were the equal of any and, in the opinion of many, superior to those of more famous firms.

It is important to remember that electric cars were always built strictly to order, and there was no such thing as a standard model for sale to all comers, as with automotive products. Each design was therefore a thing unto itself governed by the requirements of the purchaser, and while each major builder had certain characteristics by which its products could often be identified, these appeared only when the purchaser did not specify otherwise.

Starting out at a time when the long-established Ottawa Car Co. had a virtual Canadian monopoly, the Preston firm made an immediate impact with a distinctive design which became known unofficially as the "Prairie Type" because of its appearance on most of the street railways of Western Canada. This was the nearest approach ever made to standard Canadian car design, and a very handsome one it was when it left the builder's plant. It was adaptable to city or suburban use, and to various body lengths and platform styles, the variety of which reveals the individualism of railway managements for whom standardization was an unknown concept. Production ceased with the conversion to steel construction; typical examples will be found in the Guelph and Kitchener-Waterloo section of this book.

Despite its comparatively small size, the company made the transition from wood to steel construction, starting with the underframe of the cars about 1912 and extending to the entire structure within a few years. This involved a complete change in traditional construction techniques and shop organization, and required heavy capital outlay for new machinery. So great was the investment involved that several famous old firms chose to go out of business rather than meet the challenge.

In addition to electric railway cars which always formed the bulk of its output, the company built a small amount of steam-railway equipment, was a very early entrant in the motor-bus business by building bodies mounted on motor truck chassis as early as 1914, and attempted to promote the Barber self-propelled railway passenger car (1912). It also rebuilt existing cars on behalf of their owners, and

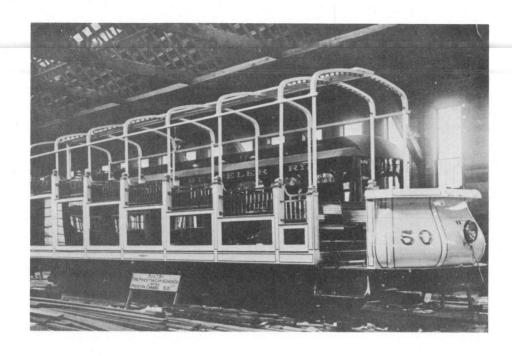

Left: Calgary observation car 50 poses inside the plant, 1912. In background is G. P. & H. 205 or 215.
Below: Preston workers pose with their products. Left are Guelph 60 and 70 ready for delivery. (WH)

constructed freight motors and snow sweepers using specialized parts imported from the U.S.A. It did not build running gear, and its cars were mounted on trucks of many manufacturers as specified by the purchaser.

Late in 1921 the company was taken over by U.S. interests and renamed Canadian Brill Co. This was to make the Brill firm eligible to bid on the new cars for the Toronto Transportation Commission, which restricted tenders to Canadian builders. An order for 50 cars was secured, built to a design developed by another Brill subsidiary, the G.C. Kuhlman firm of Cleveland. This was the largest single order ever built at Preston, and was almost

the last, since early in 1923 for reasons that are not clear, the U.S. owners suddenly closed the plant, so abruptly that not all orders had been filled; the last cars ordered from Preston (some Birney cars for London, Ont.) were actually built at the parent Brill plant in Philadelphia.

Of all Preston products, only four have been preserved in museums: Toronto Suburban 25 drastically altered as Canadian National

Above: Quebec Railway Light & Power Co. 615 (1919), a P.A.Y.E. car patterned after a Montreal design. This is one of the very few formal Builders Photographs known of Preston products. (KWR)

Below: Eight "Prairie-type" cars leave the Preston plant for Regina in 1913. Photographed on the G. P. & H. at Joseph Street, Preston. (RTS)

15702 at Delson (Montreal); Lake Erie & Northern 795 at Kennebunkport, Maine; Toronto Civic Railways 55 at Rockwood, Ont. restored to original condition by the Ontario Electric Railway Historical Assn., and London & Port Stanley 3, whose body was rescued after nearly 25 years in a Port Stanley holiday camp, for future restoration also at Rockwood. (Unfortunately no "Prairie-Type" cars have been preserved, and the design became extinct about 1950.) In view of this, it is particularly unfortunate that virtually all the official "builders' photographs" have disappeared. So far as can be determined, they were taken to Philadelphia along with many other assets of the firm in 1923 but apparently do not form part of the Brill photograph collection which has been preserved as a unit. Further information on this matter would be greatly appreciated by the author.

Equipment List

BRANTFORD STREET RAILWAY
GRAND VALLEY RAILWAY

Combined equipment list — from O.P. Maus, Brantford

Note: In the absence of any official records, Sections 1 and 2 were compiled largely from recollections of old employees, and newspaper accounts.

1: Brantford Street Railway 1893 — First numbered series

1	ST closed	Patterson & Corbin 1893	1902 re BETA
2	ST closed	same	1902 re ETA
3	ST closed	same	1902 re OMEGA
4	ST closed	unknown	1902 re THETA
5	ST closed	unknown	1902 re ZETA
8	ST open	unknown	1902 bought; named (unknown)
9	ST open	unknown	1902 bought; named (unknown)
10	ST open	Patterson & Corbin 1893	1902 re EMERALD
11	ST open	same	1902 re FREDERICK
12	ST open	same	1902 re RUBY

--The reason for the omission of numbers 41 and 43 is unknown.

BETA	Closed	Ex 1	1907 re 40
ETA	Closed	Ex 2	1907 re 42
OMEGA	Closed	Ex 3	1907 re 44
THETA	Closed	Ex 4	1907 re 45
ZETA	Closed	Ex 5	1907 re 46
EMERALD	Open (9-bench)	Ex 10	) 1907
FREDERICK	Open (9-bench)	Ex 11	) became
RUBY	Open (9-bench)	Ex 12	) 29-33
MISS BRANTFORD	Open (9-bench)	?	
?	Open (9-bench)	?	

DELTA	(ST)	No details known. Reported as both open and closed.

--Since there was a BETA and a DELTA, logic (and the Greek alphabet) suggest that there was also an ALPHA and a GAMMA but, if so, nothing is known.

MOHAWK	Open (15-bench)	Second-hand c1903	1907 re 51
NEOMONA	Open (15-bench)	Second-hand c1903	1907 re 53
THAYENDANEGEA	Open (15-bench)	Second-hand c1903	1907 re 54
TUSCARORA	Open (15-bench)	Second-hand c1903	1907 re 55

--Note: 54 may have been THAYENDENAGA. There may have been a fifth car ONONDAGA.

?	Four small open trailers bought second-hand about 1903. In 1904 spliced into two larger trailers (below)

2: Grand Valley Railway 1902 — named series

HIAWATHA	Interurban	Ottawa 1903	1905 to T.&Y.R.R.
RED CLOUD	Interurban	Ottawa 1903	1905 to T.&Y.R.R.
GALT	Ex N.Y.Elevated 1888 ?	1904	1907 re 47
PATTISON	Ex N.Y.Elevated 1888 ?	1904	1907 re 48
PARIS	Ex N.Y.Elevated 1888 ?	1904	) Became
BRANTFORD	Ex N.Y.Elevated 1888 ?	1904	) 49 & 50
?	16-bench open trailers made from two		1907 re 27
?	small cars (above)		1907 re 28

--One of these may have been ONONDAGA.

?	Open (15 bench)	3 cars, Ottawa 1904?	1907 re 34,35,36

CARLISLE	(ST)	Origin unknown, acquired about 1905. Rebuilt 1908 into primitive freight motor never numbered.

(none)	Work motor	Origin unknown (c1902)	Gone by 1910.
(none)	Sweeper	Acquired c1903	1907 re 52.

--Why the sweeper was numbered in the middle of a passenger-car series is unknown. It looks like a Municipal number, but old employees are emphatic that it had this number much earlier.

RUGGLES	Rotary plow	Acquired 1905	1907 re 10

--This number is also illogical but appears correct.

3: Brantford Street Railway/Brantford Municipal Railway 1907
Second numbered series

(G=Grand Valley Ry.Interurban car; B=Brantford St.Ry. city car; D=Double truck; S=Single Truck; O=Open car; C=Closed car)

No.	Truck	Builder	Acquired / ex	Disposition
G 10		? 1905		1930 scrap
B 21	SC	American 1913?	1907 ex RUGGLES	1937 scrap
B 23	DO	American 1913?	(1920 ex Pascagoula,Miss.)	(21 and 23
B 27	DO	B.S.R. 1904	1907 ex ?	spliced
B 28	DO	B.S.R. 1904 spliced	1907 ex ?	c1914 scrap
B 29	SO	Pat.&Corb. 1893	1907 ex RUBY/EMERALD	1916 re 40
B 30	SO	Pat.&Corb. 1893	1907 ex RUBY/EMERALD	c1915 scrap
B 31	SO	Pat.&Corb. 1893	1907 ex RUBY/EMERALD	1915 scrap
B 32	SO	?	1907 ex RUBY/EMERALD	c1915 scrap
B 33	SO	?	1907 ex RUBY/EMERALD	1916 re 42
G 34	DO	Ottawa 1904?	1907 ex ?	1913 re work car, 1925 scrap
G 35	DO	Ottawa 1904?	1907 ex ?	1915 re 80
G 36	DO	Ottawa 1904?	1907 ex ?	1915 re 82
G 37		?	1913 ex G.T.Ry. (flat)	1925 scrap
B 40	SC	Pat.& Corb. 1893	1907 ex 29	1925 scrap
B 40	SO	Pat.& Corb. 1893	1906 ex Baltimore (?)	1915 scrap
B 41	SC	?	1907 ex ETA	1915 scrap
B 42	SC	Pat.& Corb.1893	1916 ex 33	1925 scrap
B 42	SC	?	1906 ex Baltimore (?)	1915 scrap
B 43	SC	?	1907 ex OMEGA	1916 scrap
B 44	SC	Pat. & Corb.1893	1907 ex THETA	1916 scrap
B 45	SC	?	1907 ex ZETA	1916 scrap
B 46	SC	?	1907 ex GALT	1916 scrap
G 47	DC	?	1907 ex PATTISON	1914 re 214
G 48	DC	?	1907 ex PARIS/BRANTFORD	1914 re 210
G 49	DC	?	1907 ex PARIS/BRANTFORD	1914 re 212
G 50	DC		New (sweeper)	1914 re 216
B 50		Preston 1915	1907 ex MOHAWK	1940 scrap
G 51	DO	?	1907 ex SWEEPER	1914 gone
B 52	SC	?	1907 ex NEOMONA	1925 scrap
G 53	DO	?		1914 gone
G 54	DO	?	1907 ex THAYENDANEGEA	1914 gone
G 55	DO	?	1907 ex TUSCARORA	1914 gone
G 56	DC	?	1908 ex N.Y.Elevated	1908 wrecked
G 80	DO	Ottawa 1904?	1915 ex 35	1937 scrap
G 82	DO	Ottawa 1904?	1915 ex 36	1938 scrap
B 122	SC	Preston 1914	New (single-end)	1940 scrap
B 123	SC	Preston 1914	New (single-end)	1940 scrap
B 124	SC	Preston 1914	New (single-end)	1938 scrap
B 125	SC	Preston 1914	New (single-end)	1940 scrap
B 126	SC	Preston 1914	New (single-end)	1940 scrap
B 127	SC	Preston 1914	New (double-end)	1940 scrap
B 128	SC	Preston 1915	New (single-end)	1940 scrap
B 129	SC	Preston 1915	New (single-end)	1940 scrap
B 130	SC	Preston 1915	New (single-end)	1940 scrap
B 131	SC	Preston 1915	New (single-end)	1940 scrap
B 132	SC	Preston 1919	New (double-end)	1939 scrap
B 133	SC	Toronto Ry. 1902	1923 ex T.T.C. 860	1939 scrap
B 134	SC	Toronto Ry. 1902	1923 ex T.T.C. 878	1939 scrap
B 135	SC	American 1913?	1928 ex 23	1939 scrap
B 136	SC	Cincinnati 1919	(1929 ex Susquehanna	1939 scrap
B 137	SC	Cincinnati 1919	(Trac. Co. 4,2)	1939 scrap
G 202	DC	Preston 1919	New	1939 scrap
G 204	DC	Preston 1919	New	1937 scrap
B 210	?	B.M.Ry. 1914	1914 ex pass. 28	1937 scrap
G 212	DC	?	1914 ex 49	1919 sold (1)
G 214	DC	?	1914 ex 47	1930 scrap
G 216	DC	?	1914 ex 50	1917 sold (2) 1930 scrap

Notes: (1) Became Oshawa Railway 10. (2) Became G.P.&H. 39 No explanation has been given as to why, when the city took over the street railway and renumbered the cars, the numbers began at 27, nor why the city's new cars in 1914 began at 122.

KITCHENER – WATERLOO RAILWAYS
(1895: first electric cars never numbered in new electric series 1901)

No.	Type	Builder	History / Disposition
1	ST open	Ottawa 1896	1922 retired; 1938 scrap
2	ST open	Ottawa 1896	1922 retired; 1938 scrap
3	ST closed	Can.Gen.Elec. 1896	Probably retired c1922
4	ST closed	Can.Gen.Elec. 1896	Probably retired c1922
5	ST closed	?	1899 second-hand; retired (date?)
6	ST closed	?	1899 second-hand; retired (date?)
7	ST op trlr	?	(1899 second-hand (or ex-horse car?)
8	ST op trlr	?	(Gone by 1915
9	DT closed	Ottawa 1901	Gone by 1932
10	DT closed	Ottawa 1908	1938 scrapped
11	DT closed	Larivière 1902	1935 scrapped
12	DT closed	?	1902 second-hand; 1938 scrapped
14	ST open	?	1902 second-hand; 1907 scrapped
14	Sweeper	Brill 1900	1911 ex Cleveland. 1947 scrap
16	DT closed	M.P.&I.Ry. 1900	1908 ex Saint John N.B. Gone by 1922
16	Flat	K.W.Ry. 1922	Built from car 18. 1947 scrap
18	DT closed	M.P.&I.Ry. 1900	1908 ex Saint John N.B. 1922 to 16
18	Sweeper	Brill 1899	1925 ex Cleveland. 1947 scrap
20	DT closed	M.P.&I.Ry. 1900	1908 ex Saint John N.B. 1938 scrap
22	DT closed	Preston 1912	1947 scrap
24	DT closed	Preston 1912	1947 scrap
26	DT closed	Cleve.E.Ry. 1902	1919 ex Cleveland. 1947 scrap
28	DT closed	Cleve.E.Ry. 1902	1919 ex Cleveland. 1941 scrap
30	DT closed	Cleve.E.Ry. 1902	1919 ex Cleveland. 1941 scrap
32	Peter Witt	Cincinnati 1918	1922 ex Cleveland. 1947 scrap
34	Peter Witt	Cincinnati 1918	1922 ex Cleveland. 1947 scrap
36	Peter Witt	Cincinnati 1918	1922 ex Cleveland. 1947 scrap
38	Peter Witt	Cincinnati 1918	1922 ex Cleveland. 1947 scrap
40	Peter Witt	Cincinnati 1918	1922 ex Cleveland. 1947 scrap
58	ST cl trl	Jones 1878	1904 ex Toronto 58. 1925 relic.1944 scrap
62	Birney	Ottawa 1923	1947 scrap
64	Birney	Ottawa 1923	1947 scrap
66	Birney	Cincinnati 1919	1928 ex Peterborough. 1946 scrap
80	Sprinkler		1921 ex Providence R.I. 1945 scrap

CANADIAN PACIFIC ELECTRIC LINES

The roster began with Nos. 22 and 23, and seems to have numbered in both directions from there. Known orders can only be tabulated, with numbers where known:

1894: 2 cars Ottawa (1 S.T., 1 D.T. combine)	(22, 23)
1894: 3 trailers second-hand	(24, 25, 26)
1895: express car and 2 passenger cars (Can.Gen.Elec.)	(9; perhaps 20,21)
1896: 2 cars, Ottawa	(27?, 28?)
1896: Express car surmised (D.T.)	(19? or 29?)
1897: 2 open, 1 closed. Possibly trailers	

1898: 1 car	
1902: Freight locomotive	
1903: 1 car	
1903: 2 trailers used at opening of P.&B.	(rented?)
1905: 2 cars, Ottawa	(20, 30)
1906: 2 express cars	(11, 12)

From Government reports it appears that three cars were scrapped between June 1905 and June 1906, in addition to seven (probably) burnt at Preston in the fire. Old employees talk of cars with various numbers: 3,6,27, 29,37,39,49, a few of which (such as 6 and 37) seem to have existed.

After the Preston fire

After 1906, cars with numbers ending in "0" were locomotives; "1" meant passenger cars; "9" meant express cars. The existence of Nos. 11, 19 and 29 may be inferred but no confirmation has been found. Old employees refer to 11 and 12 in existence after 1906, both used as express cars and locomotives. No evidence has come to light, however, and sketchy records at Preston indicate that 12 became 30 when brandnew. There is also a suggestion that 11 became 20 which is somewhat confirmed by the fact that 20 was built after the 1906 fire, whereas the Baldwin parts from which it was made were dated April 1906. However Baldwin records state "Road Number 20" which is inexplicable, since 20 in April 1906 was a new passenger car.

No.	Builder/Year	Type	Notes
10	Baldwin/W.H. 1903	Loco	Burnt at Galt, April 7, 1918
2/10	G.R.Ry. 1919	Loco	Built with salvage from above. To 222
20	Ottawa 1907	Loco	To 224 (1500v)
21	Ottawa 1907	Pass.	Not used after 12/21; 1935 scrap

No.	Builder/Year	Type	Notes
30	Ottawa 1906	Loco	1906 ex 12. Not used after 12/21.
31	Ottawa 1907	Pass.	Not used after 12/21; 1935 scrap
39	?	Exp.	1917 ex G.V.Ry.; not used after 12/21
40	Baldwin 1910	Loco.	1922 to Hull Electric Co. 107
41	Ottawa 1907	Pass.	1919 reblt.; not used after 12/21
51	Ottawa 1907	Pass.	Not used after 12/21; 1935 scrap.
61	Ottawa 1910	Pass.	Not used after 12/21; 1935 scrap.
81	Ottawa 1910	Pass.	To 824 (1500v)
205	Preston 1912	Pass.	To 826 (1500v)
215	Preston 1915	Pass.	To 828 (1500v)

Old 20 and 30 were built in 1905 and burnt at Preston when only a year old. No. 30 in above list was built in 1906 as 12, but apparently never ran under this number as it was still in the shop after arrival from the builders when burnt, subsequently renumbered 30. No explanation has been found for the missing number 71.

1500-volt cars

(G: owned Grand River; L: owned L.E.&N.; Preston: Preston Car & Coach Co.; G.R.Ry.: Preston shops of the railway)

	No.	Builder/Year	Type	Notes
L	50	Baldwin 1915	Loco	Burnt Brantford 11/20, reblt. as 335
L	60	Baldwin 1915	Loco	Passenger gearing. 1921 to 333
L	209	Preston 1915	Combine	1921 to 733
L	219	Preston 1915	Combine	1921 to 735
G	222	G.R.R. 1919	Loco	1921 ex 10. 1958 scrap.
G	222	G.R.R. 1958	Loco	1963 to Iowa Terminal Ry. 70
G	224	Baldwin 1906	Loco	1921 ex 20. Reb. 1952. 1963 to Iowa Terminal Ry. 62
L	225	Preston 1915	Pass.	1921 to 933
G	226	Preston 1921	Loco	Reb. 1949. 1962 to Iowa Terminal 80
G	228	Preston 1921	Loco	Reb. 1940. 1962 to Iowa Terminal 82
G	229	?	ExpTrl	Ex C.P.R. 1918. Condemned 1919
G	230	Baldwin 1930	Loco	1946 ex Salt Lake & Utah. Reb. 1953. 1962 to Cornwall S.R.L.&P. 17
G	232	Baldwin 1919	Loco	1946 ex Salt Lake & Utah. 1963 scrap.
G	234	Baldwin 1920	Loco	1946 ex Salt Lake & Utah. 1963 scrap.
L	235	Preston 1915	Pass.	1921 to 935
L	245	Preston 1915	Pass.	1921 to 937
L	255	Preston 1915	Pass.	1921 to 939
L	265	Preston 1915	PasTrl	1921 motorized, reno. 953
L	275	Preston 1915	PasTrl	1921 motorized, reno. 955
L	333	Baldwin 1915	Loco	1921 ex 60. Reblt. 1952, 1962 sold Cornwall 15
L	335	Baldwin 1915	Loco	1921 ex 50. Reblt. 1953, 1962 sold Cornwall 16; 1973 H.C.R.R.museum
L	337	G.R.R. 1921	Loco	Sold Iowa Terminal 81

	No.	Builder/Year	Type	Notes
L	509, 511, 513, 515, 517: Open-platform C.P.R. coaches used as trailers from 1916 behind motor 60. Used only a few years.			
G	622	Preston 1921	Bagg.	May 1957 scrap
G	624	Preston 1921	Combine	1937 ex 866. October 1956 scrap.
G	626	Nat.Stl.Car 1947	Combine	May 1957 scrap
L	733	Preston 1915	Combine	1921 ex 209. 1922 to 797
L	735	Preston 1915	Combine	1921 ex 219. 1922 to 795
L	795	Preston 1915	Combine	1922 ex 735. February 1956 scrap
L	797	Preston 1915	Combine	1922 ex 733. To N.R.H.S. 8/55
G	824	Ottawa 1910	Pass.	1923 ex 81. 1934 retired; 1946 scrap
G	826	Preston 1912	Pass.	1923 ex 205.1947 retired; 1953 scrap
G	828	Preston 1912	Pass.	1923 ex 215.1947 retired; 1953 scrap
G	842	Preston 1921	Pass.	October 1956 scrap
G	844	Preston 1921	Pass.	October 1956 scrap
G	846	Preston 1921	Pass.	October 1956 scrap
G	848	Preston 1921	Pass.	October 1956 scrap
G	862	Preston 1921	Pass.	October 1956 scrap
G	864	Preston 1921	Pass.	October 1956 scrap
G	866	Preston 1921	Pass.	Aug. 1933 burnt; 1937 to 624
L	933	Preston 1915	Pass.	1921 ex 225. Sept. 1953 scrap
L	935	Preston 1915	Pass.	1921 ex 235. April 1954 scrap
L	937	Preston 1915	Pass.	1921 ex 245. May 1955 scrap
L	939	Preston 1915	Pass.	1921 ex 255. April 1955 scrap
L	953	Preston 1915	Pass.	1921 ex 265. April 1954 scrap
L	955	Preston 1915	Pass.	1921 ex 275. Sept. 1953 scrap
L	973	Preston 1921	Pass.	October 1956 scrap
L	975	Preston 1921	Pass.	October 1956 scrap